# Ubac and Me

# Ubac and Me

*A Life of Love and Adventure*
*With a French Mountain Dog*

CÉDRIC SAPIN-DEFOUR

translated by Adriana Hunter

Harvill
*Secker*

1 3 5 7 9 10 8 6 4 2

Harvill Secker, an imprint of Vintage, is part of the
Penguin Random House group of companies

Vintage, Penguin Random House UK, One Embassy Gardens,
8 Viaduct Gardens, London SW11 7BW

penguin.co.uk/vintage
global.penguinrandomhouse.com

First published in Great Britain by Harvill Secker in 2025
First published in French under the title
*Son odeur après la pluie* by [Imprint name] in 2025

Typeset in 12.4/17pt Calluna by Jouve (UK), Milton Keynes
Printed and bound in Great Britain by Clays Ltd, Elcograf S.p.A.

The authorised representative in the EEA is Penguin Random House Ireland,
Morrison Chambers, 32 Nassau Street, Dublin D02 YH68

A CIP catalogue record for this book is available from the British Library

ISBN 9781787304833

Penguin Random House is committed to a sustainable future
for our business, our readers and our planet. This book is made
from Forest Stewardship Council® certified paper.

To the 'Lady of the Rio Bianco'
whose leaps and falls
structure my every day

# Contents

# CONTENTS

## PART THREE

# PART ONE

# I

# A small ad

An openness to happiness or something like that.

What else could explain the unexpected?

Chance meetings destined to make our lives a better place sometimes happen on dreary days, just like that, with no fair warning. We're improvising our way through the ordinariness of a dull pallid day, anticipating nothing beyond a tomorrow, only too aware of the world's shortcomings and too unaware of our own enviable circumstances, and then a stroke of good luck dictates that it's our turn, a peculiar pendulum swing connecting the impact of an event and the improbability of it actually happening.

The walkways in shopping malls are not very elegant places, and the one in Sallanches is no exception. First, we're clobbered over the head: a low ceiling of grey squares as if the sky doesn't exist and we don't even particularly miss it. Then we're operated on, white light everywhere, stark as a cranial drill, piercing at first but eventually we don't feel a thing. Lastly, noise, lots of it, our era can't deal with silence. Someone – who's nowhere to be seen – shrieks out recipes for a better life, the same recipes for all of us; you can wander off, hide wherever you like, they'll find you. Every ten paces, things flash. All the people are used to it, and I'm one of them. These are places where humanity has relinquished all aspirations to grace, including one of its most steadfast guises: restraint. Places that have no real soul . . . but where mine will be intensified for ever.

The bar is called the Penalty; it could have been the Corner. On its lettuce-green windows is a goal, a tall, slightly balding dark-haired man in blue, perhaps Zidane, and footballs painted on in Tipp-Ex. You can have a hundred different drinks here, place three-way bets, play the lotto and buy tobacco products; it offers a wealth of addictions and there's nothing to stop you indulging several simultaneously. You're served charcoal-black coffee that the French claim is exquisite, and a chocolate-covered peanut in an individual plastic wrapper. At the bar, voices are raised, discussing suspect geopolitics; finding a single culprit to explain everything seems to make life more comfortable.

I reach for a newspaper. When trying to disguise the fact that we're alone in a public place, we alight on the first available knick-knack and pretend to have a full life. In 2003, France still had flimsy newspapers full of local ads and named after the regional *département*, in this instance the *74*. In the corners of the

4

pages, previous readers have scribbled drawings that made sense to them alone and must have made them feel better in some way. These few scant pages discuss everything, and basically nothing. I escape into them, which gives an idea of my ambitions for the day. Some of the ads spill beyond Haute-Savoie, venturing further afield.

I read with no real aim, skipping many entries, drifting from the sublime to the ridiculous without intentionally seeking feel-good items. And then he leaps out at me. Page 6, top left-hand corner, under a small spot of water that makes the words leaky, very near a second-hand Peugeot J5, full MOT, price negotiable; and Marc, also pre-owned, looking for an adventurous YM for negotiable activities. Page 6, then; clapped-out machinery, eager men, and him – sitting there, patiently motionless, deaf to all the bustle, already placid.

A dog. One of twelve, all more or less the same, save the order in which they came into this world on 4 October 2003, this world where everything begins with a birth; first appearances are a different matter. Twelve Bernese Mountain Dogs; their poor mother, a heatwave summer, twelve: six M and six F. Twelve in one go, now that's what you call a litter and, in builder's terms, the maximum load. I order a second coffee. Up at the bar, a pink woman is clutching a sort of Pekinese, and I still don't know if the thing can walk.

Thinking I can get away from the noise, I leave the

bar for the central aisle, but all that changes is the topic. Facing me is a poster full of white sand, a freakish blue, a sun-baked young woman running with all her teeth on display: The wording goes, 'Stop dreaming your life, live your dreams' – people will monetise anything. I'm not sure why – oh, really? – but I dial the number at the bottom of the ad. A call, an urge, a feeling of push and pull, and pushback too. We think we have sudden impulses, but they've germinated quietly for so many years, they know us so well that as soon as they're given some fresh air, they emerge, disguised as a spur-of-the-moment decision or a truth imported from elsewhere.

Madame Château, that's her name, replies with the promptness of someone who knows why the phone's ringing. She tells me the puppies are all still available except for one but I can be sure they'll go quickly. This annoys me slightly. I don't want to be rushed – I've had enough of this constant incitement to act swiftly – not at this stage, when the whole point is to savour the moment. But actually this tiny moment is of my own making – it can fill whatever hole it likes in my life, and at its own sweet pace. I tell her that, at just a month old and barely able to walk, they're a bit young to be going anywhere quickly, one of those clumsy offerings produced by the socially awkward who use humour to protect themselves from reality, or so they think. She responds with silent indifference as acknowledgement – if any were needed – of my superfluous remark. But I think I understand her, she's playing her part to perfection: the time has come for her to monetise the nights spent watching over a bitch in pup, the duty vet's number in her head, known by heart; the day has come to capitalise on the tender feelings we humans have for dogs. People can shame-lessly trade in love, it's quite easy even, because the commodity is so priceless.

I tell her I might drop by over the weekend just to see, if that's convenient for her. What a joker that word is, *might*; I like to think it's emphatically conditional, but it was stating the indicative with all its might. *Just to see* didn't pop up out of nowhere either, it was almost like the *I'll see your . . .* whacked across a poker table when someone begs fate, pretty please, to tilt in their favour.

I hang up and return to my wobbly pedestal table in grey faux marble, somewhere you'd want to see Sartre and Platini having a chat. A giddy feeling is waiting for me there, the sort perfectly cooked up by opposing forces of enthusiasm and stumbling blocks. I know what heading off towards Mâcon will mean. It won't be just a visit. Not a question of finding more elements to consider. Not a delaying tactic. It's provocation. Making two living beings meet and bringing their life stories together for thousands of days. You can't lie to budding love. If my white van heads in that direction, it won't be to have a quick look-see unless it's to have a look and see a reality already filled with happiness and shortcomings. And I alone will be responsible; as far as I know, neither she nor he made any sort of request.

I've already 'had' a dog. Ïko, a wonderful companion, a Labrador beige of body and darker of ear. His previous owners (that's how some people see their connection with these sentient beings – there's *master* too, but what to make of that?) had called him Ivory and then spinelessly abandoned him. He'd just been a trinket like his name, something prized, acquired by force, exhibited and then wearied of. One April morning I went to the animal shelter in Brignais and vacated a cage; a hundred others remained occupied. He was so not ivory that he didn't suit that gentle name. Ïko was a better match.

That was the start of a luminous relationship whose end I didn't think to imagine, a relationship in water, snow and forests, by the fireside, that flourished alongside life, an absolute joy that was well-balanced but not long-lived; one day, not that he made a fuss, his jaw became swollen with blood. I took my parents' car, the big one, the reliable one, and drove to the veterinary college in Maisons-Alfort, the only place that could do a scan – an investigative tool that's essential or indecent depending on the place you allocate to animals in your view of a useful world. The vet told me Ïko had only a few months left to live – dogs imitate humans even down to being riddled with cancer. What happened next proved her horribly right; vets, and this is their failing, are rarely wrong.

On the way home, sadness gripped me by the neck and I cried for four hours straight on the A6 until my body ran dry. It's good to cry, my grandmother used to say, tears kept inside do far more harm and rot your bones. Ïko was asleep on the rear seat and I convinced myself he hadn't understood a thing, that dogs had no idea of their own mortality; with animals we swear by their clairvoyance or their ignorance, it's contingent on what will protect our own feelings.

One morning, after a thousand selfish postpone-ments, love won the day over affection. I had to pick up the phone to make an appointment that would steal away one life and puncture another with the same needle, going to the vet together and leaving alone, robbed, with a collar and a handful of hairs as my only talismans. In a few centilitres from a syringe, the future's wiped out with nothing in exchange. I think Ïko was happy on our earth, we had so many plans to fulfil, and yet we knew that it's never better to wait till later.

His absence has been with me every day since, and it doesn't feel completely right to me that life still goes on. Which is why I know. The emotional undertaking involved. I've already cried with a name tag in the crook of my hand. Getting a dog means accommodating an imperishable love, you're never separated from it, life takes care of that, any weakening of it is illusory and its end unbearable. Getting a dog means catching hold of a creature who's only passing through, committing to a full life that's bound to be happy, inevitably sad, and in no way sparing. There are no mysteries about the end result of this union, and we can succumb to denial or undertake only to imagine it, but in either instance, sadness lurks, bullying us in a peculiar dance, an everyday pitching and rolling, only for joy to gain the upper hand, eclipsing this inevitable fact.

Biology, the science of life, isn't especially concerned with inter-species idylls. If your parental love is directed at your own species, the usual process of time means your young will survive you and you won't have to ravage your own life with thoughts of the end of theirs. When you love a different category of living thing with a shorter lifespan, logic dictates that the day will come when the newborn catches up with your age, exceeds it and dies. So it's perfectly illogical, it's the ultimate and a far-from-pleasant paradox that a dog's death goes against nature. The fact remains that this happiness has an expiry date, try as you might to spend each day slowing your dog's life or speeding up your own, those are the facts, there's no negotiating with chronobiology: dogs perish.

Lovers of the grey parrot have fully grasped this and spend less time dehydrating their corneas. Topstitching your life with a dog's presence means understanding that the happiness forges the sadness; it means gauging just how insoluble absence is in a sea of memories, however extensive and happy they may be; it means accepting that every minute be lived seven times more intensely than usual; it means banging your head against the seductive and vertiginous intention not to sabotage a single moment and to celebrate life with fervent intensity. For this reality and for the guts it takes to accept it, I have a deep admiration for anyone who adopts a dog.

As I walk out of the Penalty, consumed by this thought, it strikes me that it's high time I reintroduced a dash of this into my life: the courage it takes to love. I pop back in to buy one of those scratch card things; because my horoscope was lacklustre, it's the only way I can think of to tip the day in my favour.

Outside the shopping centre it's a beautiful day – who knew?

I call Madame Château back and she picks up just as quickly. Actually, I'll come today, Saturday; after all, she's as entitled to her Sunday rest as everyone else. Before starting up my van – a big dog won't feel cramped within its sheet-metal walls – I look at the mountains. From where I'm parked, the Mont Blanc chain is resplendent, the craggy Rochers des Fiz intimidating, both of them an invitation to bold undertakings.

l let my mind wander but, afraid it will come over all practical, l gently suggest it goes and checks out the dreams department.

Then l pull myself together and employ all sorts of intellectual acrobatics to crack open the true purpose of this trip – a very unequal battle. l delve into rational thinking, which I'm usually scared of. l tell myself Saturday's a terrible day for making important decisions which could affect the rest of your life. It's a day full of economic and symbolic vulnerability. The week need only be slightly burdensome, and we want our rightful share of levity, our extra helping of it's only fair, often more than is strictly necessary, to the point of extravagance.

l even venture into questions of national identity and the inglorious creeping tide of anti-immigrant sentiments. So a Bernese Mountain dog from Mâcon, now there's a foreign imposture! I've been cradled in Alpine mythology since childhood, all St Bernards, Gaston Rébuffat and the unattainable edelweiss, so for me to visit the very icon of Berne's cowherds in the modest undulations of the Saône-et-Loire region smacks of selling off your dreams and dishonouring your roots – a snow-decked Zermatt would have been a more glittering choice. And then back the pendulum swings: l convince myself it's the exact opposite. If a little distance from Swiss German rigidity infiltrates proceedings . . . well, that won't tarnish the eccentric life this dog will be stepping into. The exchange rate of the Swiss franc and my predilection for confluences eventually win me over to the charms of Burgundy. How steerable life is.

I glance at the map. Confrançon. A40. D1079.

It's not as far as it seems. And who knows, within my reach.

# 2

# Who's choosing who?

Two hundred kilometres and I reach Confrançon, one of those scraps of France that couldn't care less about the 'empty diagonal', a swathe of sparsely popu-lated land that cuts across the country, places that are charming to drive through but soul-destroying if you had to put your name on a letterbox there. Some way outside the village, Madame Château's home is reached along a winding little road whose turns serve no purpose other than to outline pretty fields of yellow-gold who-knows-what; waiting under an oak tree at one solitary corner is a Citroën Dyane.

During the journey, I thought of myself as a con-noisseur of fine books or *grands crus* stepping through the second-hand bookseller's or wine merchant's door, swearing he'll leave empty-handed, convinced that just visiting these bazaars-of-promises will be enough to fill the void, but never actually succeeding. Lying to our-selves has the advantage of being amicably forgiven, so we pretend to believe that we may back down.

I haven't called anyone to discuss the merits of this return trip and its blatant motive, too afraid of expressions of scepticism or, worse, of polite support. I like the fact that the beginning of this story is kept quiet, its outcome will all too soon be just another known fact for most people and, even though being single presents drawbacks to happiness, never having to canvass opinion from someone right next to you, never being subjected to joys or disappointments at such close quarters, is one of the strong points of singledom. I picture myself like Tintin, my only company an angel on one shoulder and a devil on the other, furiously debating the definition of a life worth living; as I remember it, optimism always won the day. The same is true of life's highpoints which recall the geographies of childhood, nostalgia for a time when dreams were valid currency, when they were self-evident, irrevocable, deaf to the warnings of tinpot prophets, of experts in difficult tomorrows, of the people we considered old. It's only later, polished by life, that we consider constraints first.

I stopped several times along the way. I was gulping down the kilometres without seeing them, my head in the air, stuffed full of 'after'. Only a wrong turn could drag me back to reality. What lies ahead is a first date, but it's all the more heart-fluttering because the other heart in this relationship isn't prepared for it and may not want it.

With all of life's chicanes, weighing up what we're prepared to lose and what we can expect to improve is a sanguine, worthwhile procedure. It's good for the heart. The world of spoiled men – which includes me – comprises two camps: those who tirelessly honour their status as living beings, terrified of shrivelling up and developing a constitutional fervour for confronting unpredictable times; and, at the other extreme, those who are content that nothing – absolutely nothing out of the ordinary – should happen to them, accumulating identical days they'll never get back and asking nothing of life but to be visible and not be any bother if you don't mind.

I struggle every hour of every day not to be like the second category, so much so it's exhausting. Does that mean I should brandish this puppy as if loudly proclaiming a constant, urgent need to live? That would mean descending into the most acute madness, an obligation to be free; and claiming that my personal whims decide the fate of other living creatures; and loving less about him than about myself. Although plenty of people see getting a pet as an aesthetic choice, like haggling over the colour of a jacket, I personally feel I'm pawning just as much of myself so I'm whipped up to the point of nausea . . . and it feels good.

The house is a large L-shaped farm, the shorter side cutely renovated and covered in Giverny tiles, the longer one in its original state with a roof of black sheet metal, dotted with occasional red, replete with memories and jumbled aspirations. The stone has reappeared on the walls of the short side; on the longer side the wattle and daub covering is standing its ground – the children want to change their parents' house, the grandchildren to rediscover it.

There are dogs everywhere here. You needn't go so far as loving them, but you can't be afraid of animals to venture on to the premises; Madame Château is protected by gatekeepers. To access the property you drive between two stone pillars topped with lions' heads but not connected by a gate; maybe someday they will be. There's no fence to the left or the right of the pillars either – life is lived out in the open here, but there are clearly dreams of an estate.

Yes, dogs everywhere! Small ones, huge ones, the barkers, the welcoming, the sceptical, some in pens, most running free, not one of them tied up, and all making a tremendous noise. Dogs born here are lucky, the place exudes a feeling of movement, of blending and of pliable rules – it's an immeasurable asset to be accustomed to freedom so early in life. I stop the van about halfway across the yard for fear of running over a member of the reception committee; as I turn off the ignition, I promise myself I won't automatically idealise everything here in the moments to come. Then I reconsider: banish charm? How stupid. Several mutts are jumping up at my door, I'd forgotten how little they care about aesthetics.

Stepping out of the van, I've barely put a foot to the ground before I'm assailed by a multicoloured pack, let's see who's first to decorate my pale trousers – a wonderfully appropriate sartorial choice – with a pawprint. They all converge on me, dogs have the gift of reminding us we're alive. I look at them one by one, wondering who's related to who, who's a bit of a leader or an elder statesman, who has always been slightly reserved or shunned; I try not to neglect any of them. Some are barking, others copying them, the fact that I'm not afraid intrigues them.

Alerted by the choir, Madame Château emerges from the house, bringing a smell of cinnamon. She immediately calls an end to the effusive welcoming; and is heeded, promptly. All the dogs return to their inactivity except for one, a caramel-coloured sort of Chow Chow with deep-set eyes which has stayed at her feet, showing off a little, perhaps the only one that's hers.

Madame Château is exactly as I imagined her from her voice, which is unusual – my predictions generally fail spectacularly. A dark-haired woman, fortyish, sprightly, the sophistications of a saleswoman half-obscuring a rural background, fists on her hips, head thrust forward. Her direct eye is characteristic of people who don't need to make a performance of character. She shakes my hand firmly, already establishing her importance. I was thinking of kissing her on the cheek. I'm wary of people who don't look like what they are, you can tell soon enough, and this woman isn't one of them. She radiates a sense of kindness devoid of naivety, gentleness without timidity, elegance stripped of all narcissism, which matters: she's the very first human the puppies get to know and I like to believe in conclusive impressions. We exchange the usual courtesies, she about how easily I found the place and how long it took, while I'm all you've got a very quiet spot here and I won't keep you long . . . but I get the feeling she's not one for pointless words, so I try not to give her too many.

'Let's go and see the littl'uns!'

I don't know whether I should derive any satisfaction from the fact that a childish expression can raise my spirits as powerfully as two lines of Rimbaud would but that's what happens, the heart is generous enough to welcome every sign that it is *fated to happiness*. I say 'I'd be delighted' or something equally old school.

We walk along one wing of the house. It's now drizzling. At the far end of the neighbouring field a whole spectrum of colours appears, a favourable sign, all those beauties have agreed to meet here, but should I hold back? We all know that when we try to catch a rainbow, it moves away, becomes evasive and disappears.

We walk through various spaces, enclosures, informal areas that seem to act as territory for their occupants. Wire fencing, but only just, less to separate than to protect, like multiple subdivisions in an improbable housing estate where no one's frightened of the neighbours. There's a strong smell of dog hair, I spot a poo here and there but nothing like the filth that some people let their dogs languish in. There are terriers, sort of poodles, border collies, retrievers, some that my search engine doesn't recognise, a mosaic of dogs with distinct dimensions, shapes, coats and personalities . . . narrow questions of identity don't seem appropriate.

The one thing they have in common is that they're all *Canis lupus familiaris*, descended from the same grey wolf. Time has worked its miracles on whims of morphology and diverging character traits, conceiving small ones for exploring underground tunnels, hardy ones for pursuing game, ones with webbed feet to save the drowning, gentle ones to guide the blind, and ones with no other purpose than being part of the world, useless essentials. All ethnicities seem to cohabit blithely here. Why is it that we humans, all descended from the same ape, are so confusingly monomorphic that we perceive such a crucial and divisive distinction in the tiniest nuance of melanin? In the taxonomy stakes, we didn't inherit the most indulgent spot. It must be so nice to live surrounded by a thousand visible singularities; we could then pursue something greater, be it in the name of humanity or following our star or another of those all-embracing ideas that unite us. Instead of which, because we're too alike, we'd rather cling to what differentiates us.

As we walk past, the dogs get to their feet, bark and come over. They look at me with their candid eyes and seem to plead. That I'll take them with me or not tear them away from the joys of this tribe, who can say?

We have to walk on a little further to see the Bernese Mountain Dogs. They're behind the house; it's the same zoning system as dealers use, the strongest substances are kept out the back. Madame Château tells me she keeps them here because they can see the kitchen and whoever's in it – the breed hates being left alone, they need people around them, any people, and they need to see everyone grouped together, a legacy from a pastoral era when they undertook shepherding tasks, rather than simply bandaging our loneliness. On the way there, just to make conversation, she reminds me there are six dogs and six bitches, a big litter and all of them healthy, vaccinated and microchipped. I say I'm very glad Bernese attitudes are ahead of the curve on equality and pandemic prevention but I'm worried that some day, at the mercy of traceability, we too will all be numbered. My hostess nods politely with a salesman's smile . . . if humour's a fortification, you end up pretty defenceless when you go it alone.

I catch sight of a tired but alert-looking bitch – I'll

discover later that she's the mother. She's resting, it's her shift without her litter of suction cups. I get a mental picture of the dogs you see by the dozen wandering the streets in the Balkans, with great swollen teats, a litter every year, the number of puppies in inverse proportion to their own strength, and their lives, their unchanging lives dedicated to keeping them on the streets. Meanwhile, the father's probably one of the mastiffs with a deep bark over there, wrongly oblivious to family matters.

Then we reach the puppy zone. It's a nice spot with the plain stretching as far as the eye can see, east-facing views on offer, sheltered from the chill *bise* wind, planted squarely on the ground and in the surrounding silence. It's good to come into the world in this powerful setting with its far horizons and clear air. They're one month and four days old, tomorrow it will be five. Born blind and deaf, like all puppies, they trust in their mother's protection and they've devoted their early days to sleeping and eating – the definition of idleness. And probably also to loving, even at this stage.

For nearly a week, Madame Château explains, they've been awake for some of the day and in these rare alert moments they take an interest in the world beyond their mother's distended belly. There's so much to discover and even their small enclosure must feel like an infinity. When they sleep it's as a haphazard accumulation cocooned in the warmth of their litter mates – the cold is their first enemy. They'll have their revenge later, never needing a stitch of clothing.

I can hear barking, yawning, yelping and whining from behind the door to an old wooden shed, it sounds like a whole swarm of puppies. I try to rekindle my resolution made a few hours earlier – not to pick one – but resolutions are like dandelion clocks: at the first puff of a happy outcome, they fly away. Madame Château tells me she separates the pups from their mother sometimes to give her a break – the puppies' greedy love doesn't allow her much respite. In passing, I gauge the work put in by this woman whom it would be easy to see as little more than a hustler pushing her stash: catnapping like a boat's skipper, getting up at the least whimper, feeding the troops, taking care of them, walking them, cleaning their quarters and other tasks that are invisible to me as a visitor. And then letting go of them.

She leans towards the door, releases the wooden catch that's keeping it closed and warns her 'children' that they have a visitor. Two mothers, double the wrench of parting. My stomach has folded in two, my heart trills against my ribs, I'm going to be shown the creature that, since this morning and since the dawn of time, has filled my every thought. I like to think that sensitivity is the most powerful of strengths, so the way I'm feeling right now must make me invincible.

\*

The door opens, the time has come for our meeting. It will never happen again.

This century isn't yet three years old, and its history is already being written. A few seconds that I'll still know by heart when all memory of the day before has vanished.

A scrum of fur starts to advance messily, impossible to tell which little body corresponds with which little head and which grunt, what we're dealing with is a single entity. It squeaks and rolls, it trips and bumps, each puppy follows another which is doing the same with the one in front, just moving seems to be enough, being together vital. What heart of stone could split up this cohort? In my family we're sports teachers and the job has developed in us a knack for quickly and accurately counting the participants in a collective movement, and for identifying which of the group might be absent. I scan the turbulent troop and count eleven players, including one with a pink collar – out of contention and already spoken for. I count again, still eleven. The scrum comes to a halt in front of the great hills of our four shoes. Still eleven. Didn't the 74 say twelve?

Dog people swear it's the dog that chooses you and not the other way around, and this is a very flattering notion. There's a sense of reintroducing a glorious animal quality into an over-regulated life, lulled by illusions of wild affinities – people who're afraid of a bit of mud still wish they were wolves. The whole idea is nonsense.

At that exact moment, the dog chooses me.

*Number twelve* steps into my life. With all the grace and confidence that comes with being expected.

# 3

# First meeting

The study of canine behaviour is a science for killjoys.

When all we want is poetry, it serves us up DNA sequences and neural synapses, pure Cartesian logic – how depressing: everything can be explained and dissected. And so, over the centuries, dogs' faces have changed and are now very different from the original solitary wolf. Two small muscles appeared around the eyes, a genetic mutation that raises the eyebrow area, widening the eyes and giving today's dog the sickly-sweet expressiveness so prized by postcards and that reels in dewy-eyed people. Using its eyes to say *I love you* is therefore just an animal's food-motivated opportunism, an astute strategy fully aware of its human neighbour's vulnerabilities. Isn't this academic version chilling? There's more to it than that. There must be.

At least a minute after the traffic jam caused by the other eleven, *the* dog appears. As if emerging from the abyss, blind and luminous. Alone, detached from the others and in as little hurry to see me as possible. An apparition, yes, let's dare to use that word, with no other idols than a belief in serendipitous meetings. Its novice eyes could alight on a hundred marvels, a flitting leaf, a brother picked at random or the woman with the familiar smell, but it's to me that the puppy grants its steady gaze, as if I were the only enigma in this world. We look at each other, magnetised, unblinking, and the child's game in which the first to look away loses – a pretext for so many budding idylls – begins, and it won't end until one of us closes our eyes once and for all. This dog will never take its attentive eyes off me, and I know that through these windows on the soul, it's going beyond seeing, it's looking at and understanding every part of me, including the things I try to keep invisible.

Do moments like that happen because we so fervently desire them that we'll reshuffle the world for them? Are they reality or our imagination's indulgent reconstructions? This question torments us humans who are so unsure of our power to knock destinies into place. Truth be told, who cares about the chicken and the egg and tricks played by the hippocampus; that's what happened: the puppy looked at me, I looked at the puppy, we told each other 'It's you' and the world tilted on its axis – one of the mysteries of a life that's beyond either of us, that's all.

*

Then, the puppy suddenly accelerates which, by her definition of urgent kinetics, amounts to walking without the usual daydreaminess; she pays no attention to her eleven brothers and sisters, unceremoniously trampling on them, one paw on an eye, the other on another eye, and puts her two tiddly forepaws on my trousers, she wants to climb me. She's still looking me right in the eye and for her, this minuscule thing, it's like gazing at the sky. For me, the giant, there's a feeling of being implored as I stand impossibly tall; I'm not used to it.

For anyone who's afraid their barriers will come crashing down in intense moments like this, offhandedness is a refuge; we can try to pluck the rudiments of a joke from the air, wielding it with varying degrees of competence, and in doing so, make an escape thinking we've retained our dignity. Few people are brave enough to reveal their cracks; some day, like adept practitioners of kintsugi, we'll know how to highlight them with gold and exhibit them in broad daylight. I'm scared witless. I clutch at glibness as if it were my final act of mutiny, wiping my eyes – this wretched wind – and blundering on with an unoriginal joke about Swiss punctuality, which has been so dazzlingly refuted by this twelfth cuddly toy. Something along the lines of 'What's all the rush, guys?' delivered in my appalling attempt at a Swiss accent.

'*Her?* I don't think so!'

Because yes, like the worst of bad jokes, I've succumbed to gender stereotyping. It's a girl, I'm sure
it is. Only a girl could so effectively exude indifference *and* complete understanding, a balancing act
that sets a trap into which we so willingly founder.
Madame Château picks up the puppy and tells me no,
it's a boy; she adds with a smile, with all the bits on
the outside. In a memory-induced flash, I'm standing
in the tiny office used by the school nurse, who spent
the first week of October dropping the Petit Bateau
pants of all the Year 8s at Lumière d'Oyonnax middle
school to check that our gonads had opted to drop.
The boy who was told to come back in March became
the laughing stock of the other young males and had
a terrible winter. Before going into the office, having
learned the laws of gravity a few days earlier, I wriggled
vigorously, and every time I saw the nurse's husband,
I blushed. There is nothing, be it happy or embarrass-
ing, that dates you as accurately as nostalgia, and it
can turn up with no warning at the most unexpected
of times.

So it's a male. Stupidly, I feel even more sure this
was meant to be. I didn't have a preference and, to be
honest, hadn't thought about it. All I wanted – and who
cares whether it was pink- or blue-flavoured – was a life
right by my side to invigorate mine by breathing some
soul into it.

I ask permission to pick him up, this creature

doesn't belong to me. I kneel down and take him in my arms as you're supposed to with a newborn. In the various stages of dog domestication, apparently a search for substitute children, along with protection against the cold, was one of the levers that brought dogs and humans together, so why not a bit of ad hoc paternity. No need to support his head, he fits within my five fingers, which are trembling slightly. He doesn't fidget or seem frightened to be held by this hand that could crush him. So bold already. Or already aware. He's just there, calm, not exhausting himself trying to please, widening his glassy eyes, looking like a rat except for the teeth except for the tail except for the fear.

We greet each other as two males sufficiently confident of their masculinity to descend unhampered into sweet nothings. I adopt the cooing voice automatically used with the young. I think I can feel his heart beating hard, if only this little mite knew what he's already conquered, those behaviourists have probably written a chapter on the myocardium's ruses (but, to be honest, if their science concludes that, throughout world history, living creatures transform themselves the better to live together, then I'll grant the greatest of respect to them). Madame Château, who seems to like numbers, tells me that a puppy's heart beats two hundred times a minute. 'Well, I never,' I reply.

*

The next moment this becomes the story of a jigsaw puzzle. Thousands of pieces have been set out on a large wooden board, and organised, linked with precision into an almost coherent whole. We're sure of what we've achieved, everything seems to be right and to fit together logically. We haven't yet stuck them fast with glue but it's a done deal, we're just dropping by, saying hello to the burgeoning new life of one dog among millions, and then we'll go back to our comfortable existence. Then someone very like ourselves gets up, strides over and knocks into the corner of the board which isn't actually all that secure, the rickety trestles give way and the pretty marquetry work falls apart. It's a disorderly mess again, it would take a long time to put it back together, and we give in to the idea that we don't feel like it. Who but an insensitive soul could backtrack at this point, who could touch this fur-clad bundle of promises, then choose to put it down and turn their back on a lovely future? No one unless the heart's branching lines really don't make any sense. And so, in the space of a few seconds, whole hours and days of resolve that we're not going to cave are undone. It's a recognised fact, battling to persuade yourself of something means preparing to stop believing it.

I put him back down with all the delicacy of a jeweller, turn to Madame Château who hasn't said anything – too afraid of breaking the spell – and ask her when. When I can come. To pick him up. A simple question, why beat about the bush? I know it's the right decision because there was no need to decide, and the waves of common sense have shattered one after the other against the rampart of what you could call a foregone conclusion.

In a month, she says. A single breath, a whole eternity, time has a way of never moving at the right speed. Without asking whether I'm absolutely sure about my choice, she takes a blue collar from her pocket and puts it round his tiny neck, our canine friends can't avoid this sort of distinguishing feature. Worried that the puppy might change in the interim, I notice he has the narrowest white blaze, but I know that even without this precaution we would recognise each other in a crowd.

Madame Château offers to take a photo, which reassures and delights me, it can be my equivalent of the baby scan picture that all parents wave in people's faces, convinced the whole world's interested. From her Polaroid camera trundles a snap of a sublime puppy and an idiotically intoxicated man; for our whole life together, he will be the more photogenic and will only ever give me a supporting role.

We're starting to make our way back to the terrace outside the house. I find any excuse to go back to the babyish ears of that unnamed creature that I didn't know existed just ten minutes ago and, who knows, may have forgotten me already. The gentle Madame Château pretends not to notice. I'm alone with him. I whisper that I'll be back, he mustn't worry, he should hide from other buyers, make the most of being with his litter mates, I'll always be there for him, and happiness is an active decision. And thank you for choosing this planet and this century. At his age, puppies are deaf, but the heart has its own ultrasonic language.

Right now, I know with my own heart that another life is coming to join me, one that will both shield my tomorrows and make them more exposed. This stupid, smelly canine that has nothing to offer the world, that others might neglect or beat repeatedly, will have no expectations and then we'll be side by side, weaving our futures together and respecting this life. The love in this instance will be unconditional. There are plenty of things he won't give a damn about – my status, my finances, my virtues and my shortcomings. He'll help me clarify the important things and together we will reduce this existence to the luxury of its essentials. He'll be there breathing wildness into my days and neither of us will ever be alone again. That can be enough to spawn happiness. Come what may, laughter or tears, honour or censure, he will travel through his own steadfastness and the ups-and-downs of my life without ever yielding an ounce of his loyalty, without judging me, ready to sacrifice his own if need be. He will raise me up. This connection is no trifling matter. I know that this life together will have its joys and sorrows but that's how it is, the road to happiness is paved with torments. There are no straight routes or if there are, they're heading somewhere other than happiness.

As I walk into the kitchen, I cast one last glance at the puppy area ten metres below us. No one will believe that he was still looking at me.

On a chair is an apron. On the table, a tablecloth with meadows and windmills. In the air, the loud ticking of a clock with its important seconds. Madame Château offers me a farmhouse coffee from one of those permanently filled and constantly heated cafetières and in a huge cup rarely used. When it comes to the apple tart, I say, yes, just a bit and I'm served fully half the thing, men have sturdy bodies in these parts – only the calves get weighed. We put together a few documents, me writing what she dictates, I could be signing my life away. I learn that the mother is called Thémis and the father Salto, an improbable ancestry combining justice and gymnastics. I ask my hostess why girls are always given star-pupil names while boys are attributed with mischievous qualities. It's a cultural thing, she replies, and if you want to fight it, you'll have to accept how latent and invisible our battle is, all said from behind a mug wreathed in blue rabbits.

I have to pay a small deposit by way of reliability insurance for Madame Château – to each their form of protection. In her personal conversion system, three letters are equal to three figures. The full price will be nine hundred euros. Nothing or a lot, it depends. The ad made this clear, it's in line with the French kennel club register, I won't pretend to be surprised. I couldn't care less whether he proves to meet the breed standard in future, but I go along with it. Like any hallmark of nobility, the pedigree leaves me cold, and I know I'd never subject an animal to the religious fervour and noisy gongs of a show ring. It scares me that the notion of purity is more powerful than that of a melting pot, but who cares, I pay. What I genuinely don't care about is spending all my money, if need be, I'll go along with it, just this once doesn't make it a habit, the price matches the goods. I could have gone back to the animal shelter and done two good deeds with one action. I could have stood myself in the middle of the world and waited for a dog to pick me. But this is just what happened, that ad snapped me up. If I could I'd pay it all in one go and bring this dog fully into my life.

'Do you have an idea for a name?'

The question feels oddly formal, as if I'm at the registry office, but zoolatry has its limits and christening-adjacent ceremonies are one of them.

'No, not yet.'

'If you think of something before you come back, let me know, I'll get him used to it, it's better for him.'

I don't know if I want someone else to call him by his name for the first time.

I say goodbye to Madame Château with a 'See you soon', when all I really want is to see *him* again and straight away, but I don't dare ask.

As I walk back to the van, I laugh out loud at the fact that I caved, and I think I'm slightly proud of it. Because, although I admire resolute people, I have a hopeless soft spot for those who stray from their chosen path.

On the way home I'm in one of those hazy states, ungrounded but anchored in reality. This always happens after a bold move: there are bevvies of favourable signs – those rare instances when everything falls into place, setting life ablaze. On Radio Inter, Alain Souchon croons about longing for ideals, then a critic raves about Jean-Noël Pancrazi who's won the Grand Prix for a novel from the Académie française for his *Tout est passe si vite* (It All Happened So Quickly). Is someone somewhere still trying to convince me we're the chosen ones and I've made the right decision? Because this is clearly a plan for an existence already amply endowed with joy, a plan to let not one minute go to waste, in which I will now be aided and abetted by an adorable metronome.

My navy-blue jacket is covered in derisory little

wisps of fur. There are white ones, black ones and a few brown ones.

Fortune rubbed together these two unfamiliar materials, and life – taken with the idea of this alchemy – seems to be asking me to do something about it.

# 4

# The right name

Once I'm back in Bourget-du-Lac, the apartment feels emptier than usual. That's down to having witnessed life. Then begins a month of waiting – the waiting is happy, impetuous, perhaps enough to fill the void but if it could go quickly, that would be good too. Wary of impatience, I succumb to its gentler associate: imagining, which somehow manages both to frustrate and delight my eagerness. Imagining warms where impatience burns. And so, as if by magic, the waiting starts to embellish rather than deplete, and the joy of announcing joy sets in.

I sit on the floor in the middle of the big room . . . and some dust balls. I can already picture him appropriating the space. I imagine him barking, running, slipping on the floor tiles, peeing on them often, knocking into table legs, collapsing on the carpet, rolling his eyes, cocking an ear at the tiniest rustle, chasing his tail, chewing anything within reach, steaming up the big window, leaving little leavings, doing all the daft things expected of him and then starting all over again. I don't know what form of vandalism he'll go for first . . . if it could be Uncle Bernard's fringed green lamp, the scolding will only be half-hearted.

In the bathroom he'll watch the washing go round and round for minutes on end, and will try to stop it with a paw, the left if the right doesn't do the trick – his astonished reactions can't help but improve my life. I can only picture him young. He'll soon find his lookout post where he won't miss any aspect of my comings and goings. 'Blue Ribbon' will rearrange the place in his own way, and we'll spare each other a house-share agreement. Soon the two of us will keep coming across each other's billions of cells, we'll look for each other, follow each other, copy each other and be enough for each other. Moving him in will involve two bowls and maybe a bed – it doesn't take much for dogs to turn our lives upside down. His tub of food will go wherever we find a space that works for him, and every evening of our lives together he'll encourage me to find its exact location. He's here, I can already feel his presence, his head pressed on my knees, his mellow snoring, his smell after the rain . . .

When pushed to a certain level, predictions can feel

physical; shamans promise that in a peaceful trance we can be in the arms of faraway loved ones. I glance at the small garden and think I can't wait, when I clearly can. They say you don't know happiness until you've lost it; I doubt that, you can also experience it as soon as its arrives.

I'm expecting nothing but also everything of this union. When the time comes for the great reckoning – let's say in the year 3000 – I would guess that, like real love, this relationship will have given me something completely different to my expectations.

Come to think of it, I should let my landlords know about the imminent arrival of a dog. It was one of the conditions before I moved in: 'You don't have a dog, do you?' I said no – surely the truth in the moment is the only valid truth? And if they'll only accept small dogs (often the way with people who have big cars) we'll be okay for a few weeks yet. At worst, we'll be thrown out, and we'll turn our backs, shrug our shoulders and leave.

To get through this month of waiting I have the perfect occupation. Just what I need.

Since talking to Madame Château, it's all I can think about. Getting his name right.

I could choose not to give him a name. After all, amongst themselves animals don't give a damn about the twee names we give them, and he and I would then escape this human habit of putting a stamp on animals. Isn't naming something the first step to controlling it? So I won't call him and he'll come to me when it suits him. Nice idea but I think it would mean missing out on aspects of our bond and I would be reduced to the bland anonymity of whistling.

I could label him X23 as scientists do with whales, overanxious about loving a creature other than their own species; isn't giving something a name the first form of declaration? It's reverse anthropomorphism, a refusal to succumb to it that keeps some people so far removed from an animal that they will never truly know, leaving the pleasures of coexistence away in the distance. I personally am so thoroughly convinced of how different Blue Ribbon and I are that I'm not afraid of a bit of fraternising, knowing it won't cause confusion. This will include giving in to our human naming rituals because that's just how it goes with us – we're born twice: when we take our first breath and when we're recognised with a name. So I *will* be choosing a name for him, but that doesn't make me his father.

I've been trawling for days and days. Sometimes I really get into my research, concentrating, looking things up, browsing, making notes, crossing off, filtering, classifying; at others, I go with the flow, and this alternation allows revelations to break through. Occasionally I think I've found it, but a slight haziness tells me I'm not quite there, somewhere there's one particular name waiting.

Naming a creature isn't an entirely insignificant business. We're only too aware of the awkward relationship we can have with our own first names, the private branding that we didn't choose but that sticks anyway; that – at best – we will have come to terms with by the end of our lives but that's sometimes so mismatched we have serious plans to change it or tactically introduce a more appropriate nickname. My friends call me Pinpin which makes me sound like the village idiot, but I prefer it to the official version.

Excavating the mood of the moment, discreetely building a memorial to our own stories, hinting at our weaknesses, sending a message to the world, setting in motion any number of tomorrows, ensuring that this baptism will have its own powerful effect on the baptised individual, inviting them to achieve the greatness we ourselves have failed to reach – choosing a name means all these things. And with just twenty-six letters.

In Blue Ribbon's case, two preconditions have come to my rescue.

The first relates to sound. It needs to be a short, sharp name which won't just identify him but will make it easier to get him back when he's surrounded by the thousand temptations of a busy city-centre park and I'm hoping to call him to heel quickly – not so I can say I'm the master but just as a potential damage-limitation exercise. It's a hard and fast rule: when you're trying to find a dog's name, don't whisper the options. Bellow them. You have to picture yourself in the middle of a huge mixed crowd (of some people who love animals and others who want them nuked) while your dog only obeys the law of never obeying you. You'll be feeling pretty lonely, yelling his dear name in the hope of his longed-for return, praying that impending catastrophes and their reprisals stay within the bounds of acceptability. It's only at the expense of such mental projections and past experience that you can ratify a find, that you can see how unfit for purpose all those pretty, affected and exotic names would be . . . so they should be struck off the list. Mnemosyne and Apollinaire, for example, which, despite all their promise, are completely incompatible with hopes of an easy life.

The second form of support comes from the France's Central Canine Society which has attributed a specific initial letter for dogs' names every year since 1926. This practice may seem absurd, and people are free to breach it, but if an owner has complied with it, you instantly know how old their dog is. We humans should do the same; then knowing someone's first name would spare us all sorts of awkwardness in a conversation when the question of age – a long-term source of coquettishness – needs to be raised but has to be silenced. The letter for 2003 is U, and that's a good thing, fewer options to choose from. Blue Ribbon was born in the year of U . . . it really is his vocation to make my life easy.

A name beginning with U, then. One that says a bit about me, but I can also hide behind it; one that orientates without being prescriptive, a genderless freedom for a little puppy who will one day weigh fifty kilos and will owe his boundless sensitivity to the magic of his name. A name that, for more than ten years and – I'm begging please – for all eternity, will gather every possible happiness around him and will make the best of what hardships are thrown his way. A name that will identify him, define him perhaps, and surely won't diminish him, a name that will be associated with mine as if tattooed on to my life. At one point I thought I'd found it – Utopia. It's a wonderful thing to believe in but three syllables was too much and, like all promising words, it sounded like a girl.

Now the first frosts have come. Living in the mountains makes you aware of the seasons. Anyone who's lost track of which month it is need only open their eyes and their surroundings will supply the date. In the autumn, green blends with copper, the sky is intensely blue, the peaks dusted with white again – colours, nuances and combinations of them, the quality of the light. One afternoon, a sudden urge to feel the cold again and the prickle of it on my cheeks . . . I decide to go for a walk on the slopes in the shadow of la Dent du Chat. It feels like welcoming in the winter. Opposite me, under the cross on the Mont du Nivolet, the natural world is ablaze, the sun giving its all in the west. This is one of the last times I'll walk alone in these beautiful dark shadows, this radiant austerity, almost hidden but so close to the brightness of the world. The local Savoyard call this slope deprived of sunlight the 'other side'. Or the 'wrong side'. It's like tackling life backwards, lying low but not trapped, secluded but not excluded. I feel I'm where I belong here. Musing on the great chapters of mountaineering, the nerve of pioneers who defied harsh north faces; and on the landlocked history of the Alps, on times when lowly people lived in the shade to leave the sunlight to their crops and give them a chance at life. There was a time when people were permanently outside and didn't fret about Vitamin D.

And then the subtle niggle that kept whispering 'not yet' vanishes, boom, in a flash.

How did I not think of this before? we always wonder when something's obvious.

A term for a north-facing slope. So clear.

Letters, four of them, like the land set alight.

Syllables, two of them, avoiding the sunlight but not the bright sparks of happiness.

Two syllables as short and snappy as a single being.

Ubac.

# 5

# Leaving home

Ubac is there in the kitchen, I could be forgiven for thinking he's waiting for me.

Peering discreetly at him through the window, I'm struggling to believe we'll be leaving together. It's him, no doubt about it, changelings have no place in this fairy tale, I recognise his narrow blaze and the half-clumsy half-feline way he moves, a rolling gait. He's beautiful. Incredibly beautiful. I watch him discovering this life; nose flat to the floor, he has a new galaxy to explore with every ten paces: a table leg, a bag of apples, two logs of firewood, a slipper, another table leg, the same bag of apples. None of these treasures is more precious than the next, the idea is to accumulate them. With every noise, he stops, wanting to understand. Does he have any idea how much there is to learn?

There are moments – very rare moments, often they don't happen at all – when life puts you exactly where you need to be. Everything fits together, from the light to the sounds of words, from human elements to future prospects. As if – despite what until now looked like chance, like aimless drifting and spectator status – everything has been brought together to offer you this scene and this role that you must grab with both hands.

Madame Château has spared me the separation scenes – from the litter, from his mother – and Ubac seems to have appeared in this kitchen from nowhere. Maybe they whined, maybe he yowled in terror? It's inhumane to tear a creature from its family, our morals and laws condemn people for as much in human society. Animals, apparently, feel nothing. It's rather convenient to swear by their shortcomings; a way to resolve plenty of qualms. After all, humans make what they want of the savage animal world: when it suits us, we elevate it to the status of a supreme and utterly legitimate model; at other times, we hold our noses at its heartlessness.

I go in without knocking, as per my instructions.

Ubac stops all his exploring and runs over to me; if he'd been given stage directions for how to get this just right he couldn't have done it better. I pick him up and snuggle him to my neck – perhaps I should have gone down to his level? – and we kiss, or something like that. His micro-tongue is as rough as blotting paper, and his breath isn't what you'd expect on a second date. With his sharp little teeth, he nibbles at my shirt collar and then my fingers which tell him a half-hearted no. He's doubled in size but I can feel his ribs, he's now dressed in a sort of wool that's coming through all over his body, his nose and the pads of his paws are sugared-almond pink, his taupe-coloured feet are sweeter still, his eyes no longer misty, and his miniature tail is like a metronome set to 200. From his little radish, which the school nurse would have rejected in the blink of an eye, he pees on me a bit, let's say it's the excitement.

My God, he's beautiful. I ask Madame Château for confirmation, and she says yes very beautiful, and there she is in her blue dress watching us with moist eyes, she'll never get used to it. I put him back down carefully, showing whomever it might concern that he's in good hands. We sit on oak chairs with rush seats, the coffee's hot, the waxed tablecloth wiped clean. There always seems to be a warm fruit tart in this kitchen, today it's pear.

'Well, here we are, the time's come.'

'Absolutely, yes.'

'So have you picked a name?'

'Ubac.'

'That's nice.'

'I think so too but it's not for me to say.'

'It reminds me of my schooldays, I could never remember which one was in the sun.'

'I got confused too.'

'Mind you, I've always preferred questions to answers.'

'Well, that's a stroke of luck, life's full of them.'

I have to sign some final papers, including a cheque. She scrawls something and hands me a vaccination record with 'Ubac' written on it; it's ridiculous but I find this moving – so far I've only spoken the name. She explains the vaccination programme to come and a few rules for the handover, including how frequently to feed him, how much and what brand of kibble. This woman's so tactful, advising without giving orders, warning without making me anxious. It's going to be great, she says. Let's hope life's listening.

Stepping into this kitchen feels like going through an airlock: I completely leave one world behind and unavoidably enter another; there's an end and a beginning, and the impossibility of backtracking. With a couple of signatures and three fur-clad kilos, nothing will ever be the same again. Ubac, as he so often will, is doing his utmost to remove any solemnity from the occasion, having suddenly focused his love of exploration on the rear end of the pet Chow Chow, his small front paws resting on its haunches while his own hips jerk unambiguously – the other dog doesn't seem keen. Madame Château and I laugh, dogs have a gift for quashing any ambitions of ceremony or helping us avoid them. His sexuality may not be fully determined, but at least it appears to be precocious and insistent. All through our time together I'll wonder whether my male companion is in search of a partner for the sake of carnal pleasure or the nobler motive of continuing his species. The day he vigorously clutches at one of Louisette's legs – she's my be-whiskered eighty-something neighbour – I'll know it's neither.

Then Ubac lies down at my feet, following to the letter the manual for the perfect adoptee. He's exhausted, having done more in the last hour than since he was born. Madame Château tells me he's already been into the house with his brothers and sisters, she does this with all puppies to get them used to the diversity of the world, the vacuum, the TV news, slamming doors and the hustle and bustle of humans. I thank her, it's stupid. What if it were up to us to adapt to the placidity of animals?

Right, now we've started our life together; which is unusual, it normally takes a succession of dates, hopes and fears, roses and poems, and a carefully implemented ratchet effect before two lives fall in step. With a dog you go in alone and an hour later you come out together. What's been lost in terms of languishing is gained in power.

'I know my dogs ... dogs in general. I can tell Ubac's glad to be leaving. I'm not just saying that to reassure you.'

'But you *are* reassuring me.'

Is it really what he wants? Is he happy with this? These questions will go gently round and round in my head for years to come and the only reply they will ever

get is my presumptuous and possibly misguided interpretation of what he wants.

'With people, at least we can be sure, they talk.'

'Yes, but they can say whatever they want.'

I'd like to talk to this woman for hours. I could be
falling in love with her, less for herself than for what
she is: love, quite simply the source of it.

I stand up and Ubac does too, following me. Thank
you, little mite, for making this easy for me, I wouldn't
have tolerated forced beginnings where only a man's
firm hand determined your fate. Madame Château and
I say our goodbyes, it's a concert of handkerchiefs, each
of us granting the other the idiotic spectacle of tears.
For years on end, I will send her photos of the dog, as
kidnappers do: proof of life.

We (yes, we) leave the farm behind. I wave a few times.
I tell Ubac he should maybe say goodbye and then feel
euphoric for being so absurd.

When I turn out of the gateway, I see that the
hamlet is called Le Bûcher – the log pile, the pyre even.
I hadn't noticed on my first visit. The word could mean
an ending, something burning out, but of course what
it's whispering is full of blazing promise. I share my
thoughts with Ubac, who seems to agree, nodding his
head like a fake dog on a parcel shelf. It's a habit we'll
stick to: discussing things. And asking his opinion.
Perhaps it started at that exact moment on that rutted

road that made his head nod? During these conversations he'll sometimes tell me he's bored when I trot out the same spiels a thousand times, but more often than not he'll indulge me by listening and agreeing. Sometimes I'll get him to say what I want to hear but, on several decisive occasions, he'll say no and I'll obey his boundless appetite for honesty.

I've put him on the van's double passenger seat. From there he can see way up ahead and he doesn't miss any of it. Everything speeds past, there's nothing to latch on to.

'The world doesn't always shoot by this quickly, you know. If you want, it can be gentler.'

They say puppies should always travel in a cage, it's better for them and for everyone's safety. What living creature is ever better protected by being confined? If the danger is braking, then we won't brake. Ubac doesn't seem to be carsick, and that's very good news because he's got the sea to visit, the mountains in the distance, the horizons, Patagonia . . . Every time my Renault Trafic stops – at a red light or something else – Ubac decides the time has come for the great crossing from the passenger seat to my lap. I think he'd like to nestle between my legs. I say a no that has a good whiff of freedom to it. So I let him come and go and stumble – this is his territory now, after all.

When we stop to pay the toll, the woman in the booth sees him and her face instantly lights up. It's because he's so beautiful. It never fails with a puppy, you improve the lives of everyone you meet, except for people made of ice; half a minute is all it takes, and this isn't a question of taste. They immediately stop what they're doing, focus on the vulnerable marvel, drop to its level and, in a babyish voice say, now you, little man or little girl, are just too sweet. Sometimes, the infatuation radiates so far it seems to gently embrace you, you manage to convince yourself that it's partly addressed to you, but this hope is short-lived. At best, you benefit from a ricochet effect of this celebration of beauty, and that's better than nothing.

The popularity of puppies is deserved, they don't waste their energy trying to please, they just are and that's enough. Beauty that isn't a ploy is a superior, exquisite pleasure, on a par with grace itself – what a lesson for us peacocks. Animals have a dazzling quality, something philosophers explore in gift theory: I didn't mean to give you anything, it costs me nothing to give it to you, don't go thinking this gift belongs to you, it can be shared by everyone, but if it does you good, don't let's deny ourselves the pleasure, and all praise something for nothing. It's a bit like *sospeso* coffee in Naples, held in reserve and offered to whomever wants it.

Often, once the cooing is over, people ask the puppy's age, is it an ickle girl, what's his name, and with a sigh of longing they say they wish they too could enhance their lives with such great company. Every time, I automatically say there's nothing stopping them. Most of them then dredge up an excuse which has already been rehearsed until they believe it. From work with no set hours to holidays with no dog-care arrangements, from a flat with no balcony to a partner with no heart . . . there's always something missing. Waiting for everything to fall into place is the most surefire way to go nowhere. A few of them, a small minority, admit they don't have the guts. Then there's one last category, let's call them insensitive, who tell you they'll never have another dog because they were so devastated by the last one's death. 'When he went.'

I've never understood how, in front of a burgeoning new life, people can talk about death, there'll be plenty of time for that later.

We reach Revard, the vast Nordic plateau above Aix-les-Bains. It's rare for there to be so much snow already at this time of year. There's a *bisolet* wind blowing, it's like winter.

# 6

# The first walk

Lots of walkers have come to touch it, roll in it and slide over it. The first snow is magnetic, unfailingly so, as if we're aware that some day soon it won't be there any more. The high-altitude restaurants open hastily, a few ski-rental shops come to life, there's a smell of ski wax and chips. Ubac's impatient too, fidgeting on the front seat. Has he already grasped that this white stuff will be our loyal companion?

He wants to jump down from the seat, and I think he may well just go for it – an appreciation of risk must come later in dogs or not be on the agenda. I set him down on the ground. He moves calmly, not flabber-gasted by the snow, one of his ancestors in his Bernese heritage must be whispering that there's no need to be afraid of it. And here I am, watching him live by my side; this is the start of a life spent looking down at the ground. I thought he might run off but I'm not worried about that now. He stops at the least little thing and stares at it. In surprise or wonderment or the pleasure of waiting. An insect covered in snow, a shouting child, the shadow of a cloud. It's a charming trait. He joyously wraps himself in every moment life gives him, utterly besotted with the here and now, impermeable to everything else. Then – at the least opportunity and with no warning – he's equally willing to break the spell and shoot off in a different direction to the one envisaged only a second earlier. He goes from the apotheosis of one moment to the apotheosis of the next, with apparently no quarter given to calculation; what prevails is the simple and unrelenting joy of existing. That's what life with a dog is like, it means relearning that an hour is made up of sixty minutes, each of which warrants recognition, and granting yourself the right to flit from one to the next, laying yourself open to surprise and uncertainty – both bottomless wells of hope.

He must be anxious, though, because he doesn't move away from my shoes. A few metres back, he was exhausting himself in the loose snow; since then, he's learned that, despite the large strides, the craters formed by my feet are more practicable. He's following me. Like a dog, morons would say. Only this morning, he still had his sisters, his brothers, his mother, the smell of his home soil to soothe him, and in a quick abduction, bam, he has nothing but me. Without me, he'd die here – of cold, hunger, ignorance. So there's a sense, a flattering vertiginous feeling, that I'm this little nestling's protector; and a sort of shame for having come through that cruel kidnapping process. It will come, it will take hours and months for me to gain his trust. Try as I might to tell him there's nothing to worry about, I know that any well-intended chatter from me will only be worthwhile if it's proved by my behaviour and its consistency. That suits me – you can't have everything with just a promise.

'You know, *someone* would have taken you. Maybe it's not so bad that it was me, hey?'

I don't know why we insist on talking to dogs. Perhaps we all secretly dream we'll be the first person in the world whose dog replies.

I let him wander, do as he pleases, I try not to keep warning him, that's the surest way to instil fear.

All of a sudden, a great Husky comes out of nowhere, bearing down on him at top speed. He's got quite a swagger, a barrel chest, trickling nostrils, it must be a male. So I'm frightened of dogs now! His owner doesn't look worried that he's seeing Ubac as a light snack. 'He won't hurt him!' Why the hell do the owners of full-blooded dogs always moo these terrifying words? The two boys sniff each other, dogs make acquaintance by the rear. Ubac wants to play, at his age fun is all that matters, he knows nothing about the vices of this world. He doesn't seem to be afraid of anything . . . either he has no sense of their relative sizes or his experience so far tells him this other dog will show clemency. Is that instinctive? If I met a fellow human twenty times the breadth of my waif-like shoulders, powering towards me and breathing hard, whatever anyone yelled about how friendly he was, I'd be petrified and I definitely wouldn't have the diplomatic reflex response of sniffing his stern. The Husky leaves as swiftly as he arrived, and Ubac moves on to something else. We – well, particularly Ubac – have successfully completed our first mediation.

On a wide white plateau there's nothing random about where people go: they head for a landmark, a point of interest. People converge on the little black ball, this tiny attraction. Even down to those who don't want to be reeled in, Ubac draws people to him, brings them together, making them happy to have found a connection. It's a delightful choreography and being his satellite doesn't do any harm, some people have dogs for this reason alone: the metric of audience statistics.

He gets called Little Old Man a lot as if life is going full circle. When I tell them he's Ubac, people ask, well, then where's Adret, the sunny side of the mountain? – I'll have to get used to this geographer's joke. More authoritative people ask what he's done with his barrel of rum, and I tell them it's St Bernards that carry those, another reply I'm learning to rattle off. Truth be told, I like the pull he has: on the one hand, living together, hidden if need be, will be enough in itself; on the other, a few public appearances and their attendant popularity polls won't do any harm in a life that's so often deprived of any sense of its own usefulness.

We're now in the woods. I watch Ubac struggling through the sloping snow. The land in this part of the world has its ups and downs. He could have ended up with a fisherman and his pond-side spots or a wine-grower and his rows of vines, but he'll be living in the mountains. Of course, I'm imposing the lie of my land on him, my appetites and their variations; the things that make up my life will shape him, I'll be a part of the determinism that I resist in other circumstances. I'm now promoted to head supervisor of his metamorphoses.

Descartes was wrong, animals aren't governed by a universal principle that dictates all their actions and characteristics. Intrinsic qualities are not all-powerful, and standing out from the crowd isn't the prerogative of sensitive, philosophical humankind alone, whatever we may claim. Depending on what Ubac does, sees and experiences, depending on his surroundings, he'll differ from his eleven litter mates with their own unique destinies, and that environment – be it full of unfathomable hopes or burdens – will have me as its primary actor. From stroking his fur to the sounds he hears, everything I expose him to will deflect him from his original absence of a plan, and I have no intention of shaking off this responsibility. It will be reciprocal: having him there will change me, and together we'll keep challenging the idea that fate is immutable – what's the point of life if we don't manipulate it a bit.

Sometimes Ubac has a go at crying. He sits down, almost completely stops moving and whines.

I don't imagine he did this with his mother – has he already cottoned on to my human failings? What's he trying to tell me? I've never been interested in avoiding difficulties so I'm only getting what I deserve, and Madame Château would be enjoying this: I have nothing but questions. As I try to decide whether this is genuine suffering or just the whim of a lazybones, the first balletic rounds of years of hypothesising take the stage. They will vary depending on my own moods but will dwindle over the course of our life together. We will get to know each other and build a common language. He won't have words but something better – looks, subtle noises, the arch of a body, the feel of his coat, discreet signs – perceptible to us alone and affording two such different beings a means of communication.

Who knows, perhaps Ubac will teach me about pheromones. Then we'll come close to otherness – not the big word bandied about to sound good while its veiled intention is to reinforce the glorious opinion we have of ourselves; no, true otherness, the one between beings so different that no part of either offers any help in deciphering the other and understanding who he is.

Back at the van, I offer Ubac a small bowl of water. He drinks. I feel triumphant for recognising his thirst, a modest reading that delights me – happiness is an art crafted from so little. If he puts as much water in his little tummy as he's splattering on to the footwell, he will have had a good drink. He's intrigued by his image in the bottom of the stainless-steel bowl, and barks at it. I put him on the seat, he's soaking and a sort of grey halo spreads around him as if on blotting paper. I hadn't noticed he was so dirty; black and brown hairs are an excellent choice of camouflage. Now's not the time to think about some day in the future when I'll sell this van 'as new'. Hasn't Ubac already taught me that the present is enough, even if it messes up our tomorrows?

We're heading for the apartment with a stop-off at the pet shop. He's asleep already. Curiosity, excitement, perhaps fear, all things that keep us wakeful are razed by tiredness. In the hopes that he'll always want to come back to me, I assume that a feeling of safety also has something to do with it.

As I drive, I assess the significance of this first day, his every shudder and enthusiasm and the strange state that I'm in myself. Taking responsibility for another life makes us vulnerable just as much as it strengthens us, even more so in this combining of lives in which blood ties will mean nothing and I'm the only conductor.

A fragile rampart, yes, that's what Ubac's arrival has turned me into.

And it's a wonderful status to have.

# 7

# Animal kingdom

The pet superstore is on the outskirts of Chambéry. It looks like others in the chain, a green cube.

As we turn into the car park, Ubac wakes, sensing the slightest change.

I go inside with him in my arms, anyone would think he's forgotten how to walk. It's not allowed but when I'm with him no rules apply. Neediness, possessiveness, exhibitionism, there's probably a bit of all of them in my decision; do I absolutely have to bring him here? From the Casa Valerio to the Eiffel Tower, I'll endlessly ask myself this question, always expecting someone to answer.

How many times have I driven past this shop without giving it a second thought? It's funny how life is divided up, we can know nothing about a world right next to our own, then one day, when we're wandering aimlessly or because we now need to, we go through a door and find out what happens in there: from practical considerations to irrepressible passions.

It could be stamp collecting, kite flying, or having dogs, life provides refuges by the thousand. And at some point in the future this other world will have unexpectedly become our indispensable exclusive territory.

Walking into a pet shop is not unlike this sort of transition. You enter the place as you would a jungle, as a non-believer, in search of a dog bone, a cat bowl or some other pet accessory, and a whole new land is revealed with limitless frontiers and its own culture: its smells, sounds, symbols, its people who aren't like you, its commerce, its loveliness, and also its ugliness which may be cheerfully masked by your initial enthusiasm. You survey this new country with amusement, relish or trepidation, you roam around, fingering things, feeling awkward. If they spoke another language here, you'd be only mildly surprised. Entering with Ubac gives me permission, I clutch him like a passport.

I do have some experience of these places. Ïko. But I wanted to close the door on them for as long as it took. Now I can contemplate returning. It's a huge store where they sell tea, bamboo cups, yucca plants, stinging nettle soup, courgette plants, lawnmowers, books on cooking marrows, even cats sometimes. A sort of mash-up between an emporium of Chinese knick-knacks and a library of antique books of spells initiating you into unfamiliar flesh, a mixture of Zen and babbling where living things are honoured just about as much as they're debased.

Green is a cherished colour here. The people on these premises think they're reconnecting with nature and its sources – a good first step or a wrong turn, it depends on your point of view. You can listen to CDs of happy dolphins and the sounds of real birds, there's a smell of Nepalese incense or the chinchilla's evacuations depending on which way the draught is blowing. Like strong spirits, the dog section is at the back – shopkeepers subject impatient souls to the longest journey. To get to dogs, you have to go past birds which hop rather than fly, then past multicoloured fish. There's a Juliette Gréco song about a little fish and a little bird that fall in love, but the beasts of the air and the water here don't seem to have feelings for each other, perhaps in the evening when the dolphins pipe down. With such exoticism in every aisle, Ubac is at the zoo, cocking his ears while my eyes are on stalks.

There's also something sad about this place. What's the point of this superstore world? The creator didn't devise these jewels for them to fester like this, confined and partitioned off; he made the horizons and the ocean depths their only boundaries, then humans caged them up without trial other than their own arbitrary vision of trade and of unequal destinies. It's like locking up the wind. Have we so completely forgotten how living things live? A tiger barb costs three euro sixty a pop – a bargain. On the label it says that's it's a fairly active fish, a good swimmer that lives in the central area of the aquarium and much liked by the 'ichthian' community (that's a hideous classic of advertising, aggrandising with a scholarly word.)

'Did you know that I could have bought three hundred barbs for a hairy lump like you?'

Living with a dog introduces you to silent objections and I think I envy the mute comfort of not having to reply to everything.

I put my mind at rest, remembering who I am outside this circus: despite the fact that I'm here now, I'm not a party to these conquests, Ubac will jump from rivers to mountains, from long grass to milky ways with no restrictions beyond our shared direction of travel. But isn't that also a cage and equally amnesic of his original freedoms? I remember a day in the drab streets of Petrich in Bulgaria, stray dogs wandered in packs, always on their guard, their coats filthy, riddled with ticks, scrounging from dustbins; while others were immaculately turned out, with shiny collars and well-fed bellies, singletons with doting owners. I wondered which, of the vagrant or the trained hunter, was the happier and whether either one dreamed of the other's life.

The dog section doesn't come off much better. People don't know what to do with dogs, reify them or deify them. It comes with good intentions and a complete blind spot about a natural elegance that needs no dressing up in frills. How very odd to choose such a distinctive creature but then refuse its lack of ostentation and work so hard to add to it. This misappropriation swings between candy-coloured cuteness and our passion for pixels, projected on to another species that couldn't care less. Displayed at the front of the aisle is the third volume of a film we should screen for our dogs while we're out. If a dog could say only one thing in its life, it would beg us to stop thinking for it. A little further on: anti-stress spray, toothpaste and tartan raincoats – clearly, without their doting owners, dogs would die of all sorts of things.

At the end of the day, this sentimentality isn't hurting anyone except for humanity as a whole, by overlooking the sovereignty of some, denying the arrogance of others, and forgetting that a few billion people deserve to be cosseted in the same way. Does affection justify all this badum-ching nonsense? We're getting into the difficult territory of inexpressible love which carries an overwhelming power: every item in this bedlam is patently ridiculous but – once it's associated with a beloved animal and we embrace its symbolic core values – we forgive its appalling bad taste.

We should walk out of this shop revitalised but are actually somehow aggrieved. Then the feeling passes and the indulgence of happy times sweeps all before it, and surely that's just as well? We tell ourselves that if everyone lost sleep – however little – over a parrot's neuroses or the pallor of a bonsai's leaves, it wouldn't make much difference to the world.

In the dog food aisle, Ubac starts fidgeting, his sense of smell apparently already well honed. I don't eat meat and yet I'll accept that cattle and chickens galore will be killed to make this precious dog's life complete. One packet is particularly attractive to his twitching nostrils, it's not among the cheapest and, according to its crowing in large print, it has all sorts of added ingredients.

'You and your expensive Swiss tastes!'

I choose a red collar out of a hundred, a brown bed mat which he will probably reject in favour of my worn sofa, and two stainless-steel bowls. There was no question of digging out Ïko's old things, this is a different story and Ubac has a right to his own easy-going life, unhampered by a predecessor.

Despite an allergy to instructions, I also succumb to a book about Bernese Mountain Dogs which points out every couple of pages what my dog could die of during the course of his inevitably marvellous life. This is one reason I'm in no hurry to announce his arrival: I know I'll be told with great relish that the breed has health problems and is short-lived. That's how our warning-obsessed society works: pessimists always seem more realistic because if you keep going on about terrible outcomes, sooner or later something proves you right and you reap the dividends. A little bag of puppy kibble completes my expedition to this place which still hasn't demonstrated whether humans are the most accomplished species or the most ill-adapted of all.

An eel-puppy and my shopping in my arms – now that was a good idea. The steel bowls clank together, which seems to amuse Ubac and the few customers thrilled that a one-man band is performing in the shop this evening . . . there are episodes in our lives when we willingly settle for approximations. At the till, a nice woman – Sophie, her badge says – asks me if I'd like a loyalty card and I say no; this will be my resistance for the day to an upside-down world in which I'm currently participating with enthusiasm.

'Isn't he gorgeous! He's not very old, is he!'

Hardly moving my trembling lips, slightly embarrassed by their own happiness, I reply with a beatific yes. I always get wrong-footed by that whole negative interrogative thing. The fact that Sophie takes an interest in my dog, it's part of her basic training, makes me instantly classify her as a commendable person; to the others, with their indifference, I return the favour in spades and view them with great suspicion. She says goodbye with a smile and says she hopes I'll be happy. People here don't seem afraid of life.

# 8

# Homecoming

I open the door to the flat for him as you might for the Queen Mother. Throw in an outdated custom and a lack of perspective, and it wouldn't take much to see this as carrying the bride over the threshold. Tears of happiness aren't far away, it's pretty ridiculous how powerful a small moment can be, I hope my life never lets me forget this one. The dilapidated old kennel in the courtyard (so there must have been a time when my landlords accepted the idea of dogs) didn't waylay him for a second, it's a given that we'll share mine.

So now you're home. No one realises – least of all us – that we'll move house together ten times.

The book recommends skilfully arranging different areas of the shared living space; making separate zones devoted to bedtime, meals, playtime, waiting, boredom, a holding area for when you come home from walks, barring the dog from certain rooms which are exclusively yours, and other subtle demarcations. This would all be very workable in the Château de Chenonceau but when it comes to my small apartment with an alcove and a kitchenette, we'll opt for mental allocations or sharing the lot.

A dog reinvents your space, putting little store by your habits, your usual traffic routes and your favourite place. Ubac doesn't go where I expected him to at all, he redefines the apartment as seen through his eyes and his ranking of what's important. I'll never tire of studying his vision of the world to remind myself that my own is just one of many options. The *lake view* which costs me an arm and a leg every month doesn't do anything for him, he decides instead that his horizons are at their widest right in the middle of the narrow corridor. That's where he slumps to the floor. Of course, the bed mat I've just bought for him doesn't fit here. I fold it in two which suits him well and he's keen to curl up on it – his way of telling me we understand each other.

What the book doesn't say but strikes me as crucial is that Ubac needs to know I'll never be far away from him, but this proximity will now be variable and subjective. It could be two metres or a hundred kilometres, twenty seconds or a week, it won't be measurable because a sense of security can't be measured; hearts that are close and mutually supportive aren't always in each other's pockets. Take me for example, just knowing that my friend Guillaume Fostier lives on this planet is enough to reassure me, I know that at the slightest setback, he'd appear from the ends of the earth; being loved is enough to make us feel safe. So I go into the next room, forcing myself not to be tethered to Ubac. It goes against nature to walk away from budding good fortune, but this discipline will only increase it.

A minute later, here comes Ubac looking for me, wiggling his whole back end as if doing the Birdie dance; I'm honoured to have become his reassuring closest friend. I tell him he mustn't worry, nothing's going to happen to him, we humans always feel the need to subtitle the obvious. Every time I get up, Ubac follows me with varying degrees of delay, we meet when I'm on my way back from just a metre away and we collide. I try not to go into hysterical celebrations every time we're reunited, I never would have thought I'd subscribe to the idea that normalising love provides it with the contingencies to drag on.

On the subject of love, Ubac now directs his towards a faded black beanbag filled with polystyrene balls that I was about to throw away. He likes it better than the floor tiles – why choose a hard life! After turning three circles, he unceremoniously sprawls across it. I imagine I should be worried about this: first he'll sleep on the beanbag, then be intrigued by the creaking sound of the polystyrene, then start scratching at the cover with his little front paws, then rip it open then eat the balls then die. But things could all go perfectly well too, the beanbag could become his faithful base camp, let's plump for the pleasure of living as long as possible with the illusion that the worst isn't always inevitable.

Next, Ubac lingers over the fringing on my grandmother's rag rug, pulling out one in every five strands with his devilish little teeth and having a lot of fun in the process – glad I didn't bother buying the squeaky plastic spinning top. This compulsive chewing definitely seems to be a treat for him; on the table I catch sight of my biros with their much-abused lids, and I think to myself that Ubac and I have a shared passion – gnawing things. The most charmless parts of the apartment now come paired with a burlesque sort of poetry; if I spend too long in the toilet according to his need for togetherness, Ubac whines, I tell him it's occupied and laugh with happiness because I no longer have to talk to myself. Then I go back out to join him and watch him transform every hour, every second.

At about seven in the evening, as dictated by the whims of civil servants, it's mealtime. Puppies eat twice a day, morning and evening, it's better for their immature stomachs. Ubac's confirms what time it is: he follows me everywhere, fusses and makes little I'm-a-speaking-clock squeaks. He's quickly grasped that his mother and then Madame Château have passed on to me the mantle of chief provider of nourishment. In the book they say you should leave the bowl on the ground for no more than five minutes, with no distractions, and if the dog doesn't eat, too bad, he misses his turn till next time. Then he'll understand that there are times for eating and times for other activities. What an arid childhood that vet must have had to take this revenge on the possibly happy lives of all their readers.

In fact, Ubac doesn't eat. Not a thing. No sign of interest. He carries on following me and falls asleep on my feet. I understand him only too well: as a child, my anxiety made me fast for two days when I arrived at holiday camp, a strategy which cost me quite dearly with the chips on Monday. We have a chat about this, about fears and doubts and the body's abstentions, I force myself not to go thinking this is peritonitis or a depression-driven hunger strike, I cast an eye over the beanbag. At the kitchen table I lose myself once more in Marguerite Yourcenar's lucid words, what a spell they cast, and she knew it. Ten minutes later my Adidas Gazelles are relieved of the small warm weight on them: Ubac goes to his bowl, stabilises his four paws, wags his lizard tail, and polishes off his paltry meal in a couple of minutes. Victory, and confirmation that peace and the illusion of unrestricted time are more productive than haste. I have my supper after Ubac has had his, which, apparently, you should never do but I'm starting to understand the book's logic – I have to do more or less the opposite of what it tells me.

*

In December night falls with no warning and clamps down hard. With it come silence and outlandish dreams, with it comes appalling solitude. Snowy, Lassie and Rin Tin Tin weren't afraid of the dark, Ubac has their moral fibre for sure. All the same, advancing implacably towards him is his first night away from home, far from his family of which I'm not a member, far from his wooden shelter, a rickety thing but it was still enough for him to feel safe. He has every right to feel lonely this evening. He most likely had no expectations of life and certainly didn't anticipate this.

We spend the evening slumped on his mat, I've come down to his level to let him know I'm here, he stretches out his entire short length between my legs, his sighing head on my lap as it will be every time I lie on the ground and he falls asleep, our pulses synchronised. I'm taken with this intertwining, these moments of calm, and will succumb to sitting on the ground for years to come. When he wakes, we try a toilet outing which produces nothing except for an electrifying exploration of the area around the house and the activation of all the outside lights.

The time comes for us to go to bed and venture into the depths of the night, depths which are in proportion to our combined fears, or to my projected fears. I'm tempted to sleep on his bed mat but that would be ridiculous, I won't manage that for a whole lifetime, we might as well start with the truth. On page 28 of the sacred text, I'm told that I must dictate to the puppy where his new sleeping quarters are to be, in a small, relatively dark space, and I'm to shut the door to preclude any wandering around the house; I should expect piercing and sustained whining but mustn't capitulate, I must brave the distress. It will get better one night at a time. *Did you know*, page 29 wonders, *that we always reap the benefits of a firm hand?*

So I tore Ubac away from his whole world this morning, instantly stripping him of his family's love, then I transported him to strange surroundings and unfamiliar smells. With no possibility of return. All through the day he's repeatedly demonstrated his courage and trust, and now I'm supposed to shut him up, isolating him from all forms of life, hoping he doesn't howl but if he does, waiting till he's exhausted to get some sleep. If he could also be happy with his lot and thank me in the morning for a wonderful night, he'll be the bestest of dogs and we can both drink to Stockholm syndrome.

At what stage in humankind's tenuous progress on earth did we decide that turn-a-deaf-ear repression was the only valid diplomacy with other living things? The fact that two or three representatives of our species pee with terror at the sight of a furiously advancing guard dog won't resolve anything; in fact, it will reinforce their unpleasant convictions. Never mind, for the duration of that terror they will have experienced several seconds of powerlessness and anticipated their imminent deaths . . . and fear will have briefly switched camps. I feel the same guilty pleasure every time a toreador, in the name of tradition, has his gilded finery punctured. There must be some middle ground between my Rousseau-inspired angelism and this instinct for domination, a space where we can live together.

I'd prefer to try freedom for this probationary night. My parents and my up-bringing full of outdoor games have equipped me to fight the notion that being accustomed to freedom affords more losses than gains. So I leave the new bed mat at the end of his favourite corridor with one of my old T-shirts by way of a lucky charm. After a lot of physical contact between us (now, there's an angle for a reconciliation with the book which seems to believe in the comfort of touch), after I've promised him countless moonlit nights together, I head off to my bedroom just like on any other day, feigning indifference, and go to bed. Let him wander where he wants and explore whatever takes his fancy, let him have the intoxicating feeling that he can go anywhere, and the freedom will paralyse him.

At first and for quite a while, I can hear his exploratory movements, many of which pass the foot of my bed, a few whimpers, and some attempts at mountaineering. He settles there for many long minutes. If one of these days a young woman joins me, I'll have to explain to Ubac that there are variations even in the concept of freedom. Having satisfied himself, or so I imagine, that any exit from this room will necessarily pass his own bed, I hear him return to his quarters at about midnight.

During the night I visit him with cat-like tread. He's sleeping and seems determined to stay asleep right through till morning. There's a slight smell of urine but who cares, there are few more peaceful sights than an animal at rest.

# PART TWO

# 9

# Life with a dog

Anyone would think it's Christmas. I get up early, eager to see what the night has brought to my life, like those nights of trepidation that aren't worth prolonging. I'm reacquainted with the feel of households that had dogs. As a child I longed to have one and found every possible way of telling my parents, from hints to blackmail, from winning first prizes to rages, but it wasn't going to happen, cats were better suited to their appetite for few constraints. They now know: only a long life proves that our childhood dreams weren't just fads.

Some animals were there in passing. Occasionally a colleague of my parents would visit with a dog: I remember one called Hawaii. He wasn't allowed beyond the garage; I joined him and we excitedly combined our happy solitude there. He was a Briard with a very curly coat, and I believed so completely in the power of dogs that it seemed obvious to me that this was why his owner's name was Mouton, which means sheep. At the end of the evening, this wiry, muscled man of the mountains, deeply tanned and lightly inebriated on Suze, took his dog with no need for a leash and left in his ancient white van that spluttered haltingly to life, and their existence seemed to me about as good as it gets.

There were other times I had a taste of the joys of dog ownership, when I went to stay with people who had dogs. The world fell into two categories: families with dogs and those without. Grandma Nounoune had Tania, my godfather had Socrates, and Auntie Marie-Françoise had Shadok. At her house I would wake as early as possible when my cousins were still asleep; there was a strong smell of coffee and of last night's burnt supper (my aunt didn't know this, but she was nicknamed Mrs Charcoal), and the radio burbled quietly in long complicated words about serious problems. I scrounged some time with the grown-ups and, more importantly, would seek out the dog who seemed thrilled that someone was taking an interest in him so early. He lay Sphinx-like while I sat cross-legged, golloping down bread and jam, and we'd talk for hours, on subjects far removed from chitchat about what I wanted to do when I grew up or what my girl-friend's name was.

When the grown-ups went to another room, he was allowed some honey on butter on bread on my fingers: I gave him the silent doughy part of the bread, begging him to swallow it quickly and not lick his chops. If the weather was nice, and that's an inexact science around the river Scheldt, we'd run out to play, inventing armies of enemies and always winning. We'd arrive back all brown and green – the grown-ups sighing that we'd never get clean – me with scabs on my knees, my hair stuck down with sweat and dog kisses, both our tongues lolling out . . . and we'd fall asleep on the ground.

These dogs from my childhood were in my gang of best friends, and – in my child's mind – being with them meant doing whatever we wanted. As far back as I can remember, I made a point of spending time with dogs. I think Shadok liked me. He sometimes ran away from my aunt's house and would come to find me, trotting along the pavements and side streets from Aulnoye to Berlaimont, three kilometres away. One happy July morning I was watching him come over when he impatiently crossed a road and a car hit him; there was a loud sound of braking and the thud of impact. He flew into the air and then under the wheels. My parents carried him into the garage, blood spreading under him. He'd been crushed and was howling, howling blue murder you might say. And wherever I went, he kept his eyes on mine. My mother ordered me away to the kitchen and I resented her for thinking of me in that moment. To this day that is my most painful memory of a life ending abruptly. Just one breath earlier there'd been all the anticipation of being together.

*

Ubac is here. He's beaming and immediately starts jumping around. Puppies are never 'not morning people'.

A dog's heart doesn't need cranking up, it's instantly and constantly at full tilt, bursting, love is there the moment they wake; perhaps this deep-seated vitality is what exhausts their hearts and shortens their lifespan. Some would say that happiness comes easily to them, they know no anxieties or demands, but that would take very little account of the emotional strength animals have. For weeks now we've experienced these outpourings of joy, their immediate intensity endlessly repeated and never blunted. Standard fare for a budding idyll, some would say.

We're establishing a routine: we have our reunion in the corridor, greet each other with lots of rubbing and stroking, go out for some fresh air, then I drink a cup of tea and he eats. We have our points of reference and our rituals. I've opened my life wide to let Ubac in and give it some variety, and here I am delighted that our mornings are all alike. In the evening, he eats again and at two different speeds like any self-respecting dog: greedily, head down, not bothering to chew or breathe – it could be caviar or pebbles – and then as conscientiously as possible, with the tip of his refined tongue, chewing the last three bits of biscuit meal down to sand as if regretting succumbing to such voracity at the start of the meal.

Ubac has grown. From extravagant growth-spurts to elegant adjustments, he's conscientiously followed his weight curve, every day differing from the one before. We've already doubled his rations, put two collars on the scrapheap, and his milk teeth have ended their brief lives in one or other of my sweaters. His skin has toughened, his bobbly fluff has recently transformed into a silky pelt except around his rear end where it's exercising his right to stay puppyish. His tadpole-grey eyes are now muted tawny marbles. His blaze has grown narrower still, he now has an almost completely black forehead and the clear expression of all attentive creatures, his whole body focused between his heart and his eyes. Everything about him seems poised, he puts a lot of casual elegance into his every move. He's a big animal, his head is huge; I like resting mine on it, he could disfigure me with two snaps of his jaw.

Ubac is still called Ubac, but also Loulou, Babac, Bouboule and other roly-poly nicknames; sooner or later, big dogs are given names that relate to their bulk. When I do call him Ubac, it's not always a good sign. I need to be careful not to keep his real name exclusively for rebuffs.

I photograph him from every angle. I often wonder what the point is – a photo's two dimensions will never match the soaring reality – but what besides these satin-finish bits of paper will there be to rekindle memories some day. And I write about him. A few words every day, and for major incidents. Just enough. Not doing this would be just living. And too many words would mean forgetting to devote time to him.

Since his arrival, we've celebrated his birthday on the fourth of every month. Having a dog narrows time and turns its rhythms upside down. It's both pleasurable because you miss nothing, and terrifying because it's precisely the limited nature of the whole thing that prompts you to notice every moment. Today is the fourth of June, he's eight months old and I've made a point of wishing him many happy returns. They say that dogs age seven times faster than we do and I celebrate his birthday twelve times more than I should so I'm only out by fifty per cent.

Ubac marvels at everything, a caterpillar, the wind in the trees, the things we've stopped seeing. He never ignores anything that could enliven his existence. His facility for wonderment is an antidote to world-weariness. Life needs no bells and whistles, it's vital enough as it is; every grouch should spend an hour with a dog. He plays from morning till night, with anything and everything, a lizard, a cork, something imaginary. What stories does he make up in his head? He's the biggest fan of playfulness I've ever met. In the grimmest of settings, he always finds something to cheer himself up. I've seen him anxious, but never gloomy. In the most formal surroundings, he'll roll and hurtle and jump, dogs don't give a damn about etiquette and will always have something better to do than pretend. These digressions of his are fun and infectious, and I try my best to adopt his freedom; it's very good for the heart to be in the company of a creature so open to everything that you'll never surprise it by venturing to do the same. In fact, I've never understood this classic statement from couples with decorous children and well-kept lawns: 'All we need is a dog,' they coo as if having one were the ultimate accessory in an orderly life. Because the truth is it's the exact opposite: a dog makes a mess of everything.

And this characteristic doesn't seem to be waning – the book refers to neoteny to explain this elastic puppyhood (the author's doing better now, apparently unconcerned that a life might be devoted indefinitely to play and ill-discipline). I'm always slightly wary of texts that describe eternal youthfulness and incite us to keep returning to it. Age and its partner in crime, experience, don't come freighted with decline alone. Along the way, we pick up some discernment, some free will and other forms of vigilance that don't stunt our lives and that make us a little more ourselves without necessarily silencing our rebelliousness. But when I watch Ubac, I notice that what we need to hold on to from childhood is its very heart: the naive enthusiasm, the dedication to playing and the non-negotiable illusion that it will last for ever.

*

We go for walks. A lot. Sometimes for days at a time. We walk, stop, lie down in the grass, paddle in the river, have picnics, wander aimlessly, all simple pleasures that people enjoy when they're just grateful to be alive. That's also part of walking with a dog, getting away, going to immutable places, waterfalls, forests and ponds, and not really knowing if it's 1950, the Middle Ages or, with a bit of faith in the survival of the elements, 3018. We're not really going anywhere or trying to get away from anything. Having a dog as company makes nothing feel excessive – not time or space. It's not even about passing time, but being of it.

On these walks Ubac meets other animals but it's as if they've already met. Only their speed sometimes surprises him: Ubac comes across a lizard, a field mouse or some other ground-dwelling creature and lifts his head to check that I've seen it too and we're sharing this moment of wonder. When he looks back at his find, he can't understand why it's not in the exact same spot and turns to me again to make sense of this. I laugh at his ingenuousness but envy his conviction that every time we're dazzled by something the moment warrants the world coming to a standstill. The field mouse – already 500 metres off to the left – doesn't appear to subscribe to this suspension of time, a notion that Ubac will never abandon and which may well partly explain why he loves slugs and snails.

I take him everywhere. Into the wild, into bistros.

Sometimes it's straightforward, sometimes far-fetched. When somewhere is out of bounds for our four-footed friends, I deduce that it's not worth visiting, it must be the most boring place in the world. If a waiter brings a bowl of water for Ubac, the whole establishment is worth the trip. I offer my days in their entirety to my dog: I don't want anything to put him in a panic, not the fishmonger yelling in the market nor the endless silence of reading.

I've always admired seeing someone go into a shop while their dog waits patiently outside, and then they leave together perfectly normally. I'm working on it. I order my baguette almost over my shoulder and call out to the baker that I'll be back straight away. With food shops, thanks to the reward when I come out, we're making progress . . . with bookshops not so much. I even take him into my lessons and the students call him Tupac like the king of rap Tupac Shakur – he's the king. The day the inspector comes in his tie, I'll have to warn the schools that are in favour of my classroom assistant not to shop me by asking where he is.

We do a lot of experimenting with untidiness, and danger too – without these things, would we ever be able to discuss love? I like the idea that we'll always be together, we're building a trove of little adventures, Ubac gives my life space, I already have memories, places that I associate with him, successions of moments – some short, some very long – and I don't yet know what will be left of them. The future feels radiant, I could nestle in the comforting feeling that my best years now lie ahead, but I'm far too busy with the joys of right now.

To help us learn about separation, I sometimes leave Ubac with friends. Every time we're reunited, I pretend I haven't been worrying that something's happened to him and that he loves someone else as much as he does me.

My life is wonderful at the moment, and there's actually nothing to dictate that it shouldn't be. Good news keeps popping up as if being happy gathers up all the good luck strewn around. Or is it a more nuanced sign that my pretentions are falling away? I have no idea and couldn't care less, you can extinguish happiness if you over-scrutinise it; that's just the way it is and I love it.

For several months I've been testing how having a dog puts your social life through a mangle.

A life weighed down by logistics because my schedule has to be amalgamated with his, his toilet-break thresholds and his profound dislike of being alone; but a life that also feels lighter thanks to the welcome moments of sanctuary when, on a woodland trail or on the banks of a river, we find a thousand reasons to leave the world behind.

A life with blurred social interactions in which I'm

required to observe, adapt and label: who among my friends is glad to see a dog sharing in our common interests, who finds his company inappropriate or repulsive, and who has the worst possible response – they don't even notice. But a life that's also brought into sharp focus because just having Ubac around is a wonderful way of screening out anything dragging me down, the pebbles in my shoe which, on my own, I would experience as boulders. So yes, I turn down pleasures that were a necessity yesterday but I'm not abandoning them, I'm just letting them lie fallow. I may be wary of exclusive passions that burn everything in their path, but right now I'm surrendering to the luxury of a preference.

Ubac and I come across a lot of other dogs complete with owners. I always wonder what form their love takes, whether they talk to each other and whether they too are convinced that their relationship is unlike any other.

Among them there are grannies with toy dogs, women whose excessively rose-tinted adoration borders on the ridiculous and strains the very definition of love. When they see Ubac, they drag away their little treasures done up in pearls and frock coats, and everyone screams. There are far-right extremists in bomber jackets to hide the muscles they don't have, saddling their dogs with them instead and thinking everyone will believe they're equally powerful. There are shooting enthusiasts who confine their dogs to two square metres of wire mesh and take them out on killing days. There are the people who put their dogs in bandanas and let them sit up on chairs, mistakenly confusing this parading of their feelings with any true intensity. There are those who venerate animals as models for humanity, believing them superior to the human race in all ways and for all time, forgetting that this automatic celebration corrodes just as much as it champions – nothing can be at the very top or the very bottom.

Do I have the right to assert that I love my dog any better? I think there are too many of these mirror-pets, pets whose owners insist they adhere to their definition of a perfect world and elect them – the owners – its worthy ruler. And this is from the man who, at every possible opportunity, takes his dog named after a mountainside up into the mountains and is at his happiest when people are flabbergasted to find him and his unusual partner on improbably vertical slopes, eschewing a lead and loving a length of rope.

One day I publicly acknowledged all this, telling Ubac, 'You know, we get dogs so you rub us up the right way!'

I was quite pleased with the turn of phrase. Ubac lifted his leg and that was that – a dog never bothers with the last word but has no trouble shutting you up.

Luckily, there are the others, the majority. They love their dogs for who they are, living creatures so close to and yet so detached from themselves, and from whom they expect no greater flattery than the unforced enjoyment of their time together.

Last of all, there are the people who sit on the ground, on the margins of a life that keeps knocking them down. Under their stinking, shared duvet they ask for spare change to drink away the boredom and feed a Belgian sheepdog, one that watches over them like the vulnerable lost sheep that they are. They have nothing in common with the Bichon-owning bourgeoisie – who are probably disgusted by them – except for their love of dogs, an affinity that is greater than all the incompatibilities in the world.

# 10

# A good dog

For weeks now much of my life has been devoted to Ubac's training.

I don't know whether *training* is the right word, let's call it an ambition to provide us with some characteristics of an easy life, a minimum of orderliness to avoid havoc. I've pared down my objectives: for him to be house-trained, for him to come back more or less when I call him and for him not to jump up at people because this eruption of affection is invariably addressed to people who are frightened, wave their arms and scream, and the net result is that they take even more pleasure in loathing dogs. And all without too many commands, for him just to know rather than obey – that's the ingenuous notion I have of our relationship.

It's increasingly successful. We're getting better. I have boundless patience in everything that relates to him, and he seems to want to make my life easier. Sometimes he's brilliant – if M had been the letter for his year of birth, I'd have called him Mr Sheen. Every bit of progress is celebrated appropriately. Other people say Ubac's an easy dog; I prefer intelligent. Sometimes we walk along the shore of the Lac du Bourget without triggering a mass brawl or new local by-laws. That's an achievement because there are lots of retired people in the area who turn the slightest blip into a cataclysmic event, people unfazed by the essentials in life but embittered by pointless details. I've never understood why at an age when people have inevitably experienced great suffering, or at least the fear of it, they don't treat every minor upset with an exemplary couldn't-give-a-monkey's attitude . . . I'd even go so far as to call it wisdom. But there are days, preferably when I'm in a hurry, that are a disaster, nothing works: there's an ever-increasing gap between my calling and his reappearance, and I start wondering whether the frequency of my voice is satisfactorily adapted to the physiology of his ears.

One of my few convictions is that adolescence isn't peculiar to humans. I've already had to run after him to show him I was annoyed, and he absolutely loved this performance. I've hauled at things that he didn't want to give back, and he's gone into full tug-of-war mode. I've hidden behind bushes and imitated whimpering, hoping he'll be worried by my disappearance, without noticing that other people were watching me carefully. I've praised him every evening, out in the snow in my underpants, for two blobs of poo that he'd forewarned me about, withheld and then expelled once outside; I jumped about and whooped with joy, congratulating him with the energetic patting that's appropriate for each of his successes, setting off all the movement detectors on the building to give my suspicious neighbours a stunning son et lumière. When I needed to pick up a couple of other poos, I snuck off in the morning for fear he would think I loved this Easter egg hunt. I've made all the usual mistakes, done a lot of stooping and scooping and we're growing up.

I'm learning as much as he is. I try to be fair and consistent and to keep things in proportion – the vocabulary for good policing. I believe in praise rather than sanctions; my experience as a teacher has proved the virtues of the one and the need for, but the limitations of, the other. This is all the truer with dogs: punishing undesirable behaviour won't magically produce the desired effect, their heads full of daydreams aren't good at making deductions. I'm feeling my way, but I don't beat him or banish him. They say the worst punishment for a dog is to be shooed away. Get lost! I'll never say that to my dog, what if he obeyed?

If I stay inside when I put Ubac out, he sits down straight away and stays there like a lump – a garden half a metre square would be enough. He sits motionless against the wall, proud and upright, braving everything the world throws at him. He backs up to the wall till he's almost part of it, pushing the full length of his spine against it right up to the back of his head. I think he believes this genie-summoning rubbing will open an invisible trapdoor in the bricks. The weirdest thing about it is that it works, a door appears fairly reliably and its latch looks remarkably like my approach. Then he can indulge in his favourite sport which I can't complain about: reducing the distance between us as much as possible.

I often wonder how Thémis, his mother, would manage surrounded by a litter of twelve learners, how things work au naturel. I think she would scold hard and swiftly, not wasting time with gradual warnings and provisional authorisations. I've seen for myself how effective it is when I've shouted because I was frightened, for example when Ubac launched himself halfway across a street as if cars hadn't been invented: he stopped dead, realising we weren't playing now and paralysed by my fear. When will he grasp that he's mortal?

I've also learned from children. On several occasions I've been staggered by how well Ubac obeys their piping voices. Using human reasoning, I thought he genuinely wanted to please them because, according to the book, a dog understands perfectly well what status of person it's dealing with. In fact, it's not that; he obeys because there are no misgivings in a child's orders. Children believe they are all-powerful, they're protected from self-doubt; when they tell Ubac to sit, the possibility that he won't doesn't occur to them. Ubac sits. I now apply their dogma: you have to believe. In what you say and what you do and the requests you formulate. Basically, in who you are.

One Saturday, more out of curiosity than because I was a convert to the concept, I went to watch a dog training session on the far side of the Mont du Chat tunnel. The place was packed with lots of different dogs and people from all walks of life, in anything from cargo pants to loafers. The dogs looked happy to be regimented (some soldiers are too). Iterations of the command 'stay' reverberated and it sounded like the exact opposite of why dogs come into our lives.

An instructor with a strong whiff of testosterone about him came over to me and talked up the classes. Of course, Ubac gave the man every reason to suppose that he would need an extensive curriculum. All the guy could talk about was anarchy: the fundamental anarchy which made all dog–owner relationships unviable, anarchy as it occurs in the natural world, the anarchy that's no longer fashionable in today's society, if you know what I mean . . . I found it all pleasingly quirky, unexpected and appealing, must be a new trend, half martial and half let it all hang out. I obviously looked as if I didn't understand a thing because he set about explaining it another way: it was about establishing order between me, the dominant party, and Ubac, the dominated one, about a system of management, fear and kicks up the arse. I gradually realised that his pedagogical devotion was for hierarchy. We were never going to get along. I said a polite goodbye.

I regularly have to remind myself that Ubac doesn't speak French. Telling him in a gentle voice that I'm not particularly pleased he's ripped the wallpaper in the hall is only passably effective; he seems more receptive to form than content. I think Ubac now knows he's called Ubac, his strength is to forget the fact at the right moment. He knows that coming back to me isn't necessarily less interesting than the new piece of land he was planning to explore and that sitting promptly can afford him a treat, including a peanut. I started with grapes, thinking they were preferable for a dog with an athlete's body, until the vet told me there was nothing more toxic for his kidneys and they could have killed him. 'We think we're doing the right thing . . .' he said. Exactly. As for greeting people's behinds, I initially told him this behaviour was forbidden with every man, woman and child on every occasion, but seeing he's now more specific, I encourage him to sniff the backsides of anyone who thinks theirs is above such things and far superior to other people's rear ends. To date, this has failed.

When I sit at the table to eat, Ubac sits very close to me and stares at me unwaveringly, only a few swallowing sounds reassure me he hasn't fossilised. I'd like to put this down to adoration but if I sit in the same place to read or write, or at a time when there's no smell of food, his love dwindles markedly to the point of extinction. When he eyes my plate, I can choose between three methods to break the spell. The first is to give him something straight away so the whole thing's over and more or less on my terms; this doesn't work well, the tinker resets the system so we're back to square one. The second is to wait till the end of the meal so that he understands all preliminary efforts are pointless; this is hardly any better, he sits there waiting with good reason, which has proved a very effective way of increasing his endurance for sitting motionless and his ability to produce strings of drool. Lastly, I could not give him anything, but the person that I am – brought up on a diet of Pierre Mauroy's socialism and of shared assets, however hard they may be to digest – would never recover. So I eat, you eat, we eat.

That's more or less what our life has been like for several months of happy trial and error. Two distinct species coming closer to each other, finding out about each other and growing intensely fond of each other, a symbiosis that biologists quite rightly call vitality.

Ubac is a good dog, goodness personified.

I wish I could claim it was partly down to me, but it's less to do with me than his nature. Any sort of tension, even the most fleeting, makes him uncomfortable, he wants happiness and serenity everywhere, and strives to protect the whole world, starting with vulnerable people – he can spot a mile off and immediately focuses all his attention on them. It doesn't matter how often I tell him that people who soak up pain dry out faster than other types of sponge, he doesn't care. The people who say he's easy also say he's a good sort. I hate this appraisal for a dog or a person; it implies a heaven-sent goodness when it's really a supreme strength. Kindness, which can so readily be ridiculed, takes a lot more moral fibre than crabby overreaction.

I don't know where he gets it from – Thémis, providential luck, or our shared values – but Ubac's humanity isn't vapid, it's intentional and resolute. It's an active choice. When he goes into a room, he can tell instantly whether the mood is harmonious or awkward, I actually think he gauges it, something in the air informs him and, using his own secret conjuring trick, he recalibrates it, making it replete. His presence alone is a comfort, he absorbs any animosity and, filtering it through invisible gills, emits it as joy – I hope it doesn't leave a toxic residue. Surprised to find everything's fine, people who don't know about dogs must wonder exactly what aspect of their lives has suddenly been resolved.

If there's not only tension in the air but also a row going on with no resolution possible, he'll go from camp to camp like the Greek *spondophores* and announce a sacred truce. More often than not, the warring parties comply, everything settles and unwinds. Alain, a distant uncle and mischievous radiologist, says that Ubac is the family's betablockers – I'm not sure whether he's referencing lowered blood pressure or stopping us verbally beating one another up, but I think I can guess. People often thank me for Ubac, as if I have something to do with it.

Sometimes, though, he overestimates the degree of distress.

One morning at Christmas time at my parents' house in Boulieu-lès-Annonay, I wake early, true to family tradition, and Ubac isn't around. I ask Jean-Pierre, the man who raised me and whom I call my father, if he's seen him – he hasn't. Disasters always start like this, having more people around facilitates negligence, we all think someone else is in control. I look for him everywhere, calling: the garage, the house, the garden, the street, the neighbourhood, concentric circles of anxiety. I head into the village, picturing the worst possible scenario, hollering his name loud and often, with unshakeable images of Shadok in my head.

As I turn a street corner, I see my mother on her way home from buying the bread and wearing that fixed smile of hers intended to convey peace of mind, but everyone knows means absolute terror. She's walking hunched over, holding a lead improvised from a patisserie's ribbon and tied around the neck of a dog with no collar but apparently very happy with his world. In the middle of the village, she sensed a presence at her feet, turned around and to her surprise – her amazement – saw Ubac. Unbeknownst to her, he'd been following her. He must have seen her leave the house and, on his scale of relative dangers, she'd represented a vulnerable, old, lone female gone astray. He crossed a main road along whose verges bunches of roses are laid every year, two busy streets and other danger zones. Alone. The retroactive fear almost makes me scold him, but I don't, I know he isn't equipped to associate two unconnected incidents. I simply make it clear that, although I like our life together being devoted to high jinks, I'm begging him, please, to make sure he doesn't die. I thought I'd lost him and, as if the point needs proving, I grasp the fact that life without him is unimaginable.

I don't immediately tell my mother because the comparison is problematic, but this saviour-of-the-world episode with its commendable intentions and potentially disastrous repercussions reminds me of an incident that had happened a few weeks earlier when Tex Avery seemed to have momentarily taken over my life. Ubac and I were walking along the side of a major road, and he saw a snail that was in the final stages of crossing, a feat it must have embarked on, at a guess, the previous morning. It had miraculously survived.

Aware of how dangerous it was for a snail to be pootling over the tarmac, Ubac picked it up in his mouth and, without damaging any part of its shell, took it safely back to the other side of the road. Two days out, five seconds back.

Once it had been gently set down, the snail – which had retreated into its shell in transit – all but shot back out, wielding furious tentacles, and I thought I could sense from the far side of the road that it was livid to have to undertake its transatlantic feat all over again. We should have let its family know it would be a little late. Meanwhile Ubac was rather pleased with this repatriation on health-and-safety grounds. I told him he'd done well because he'd clearly wanted to help, but I wasn't sure he now had a great reputation among the snail population. When he was well ahead, I nipped back to the snail and returned it to where we'd found it – none of its friends would ever believe the travels it had been on. I still don't know how to tell my mum this story without upsetting her. Bide my time probably. Or tell her it was the main road that reminded me of it.

The evening after my mother's bread-buying episode we're celebrating Christmas Eve as a family, and that naturally includes Ubac. My parents have wrapped a bone in festive paper for him and put it under the tree. Ridiculous but vital. He sniffs it dutifully, probably wondering what the point is of concealing presents. I don't know why but the conversation turns to the death of Princess Diana. My relative indifference to what's anyway old news combined with the effects of an excellent Clérambault rouse my sister-in-law who's very sensitive to the fate of princesses.

'Right, so you don't give a damn about Lady Di, the mother of two children?!'

'To be honest, I wasn't devastated . . .'

'Well, what the hell *would* devastate you?'

'If my dog died.'

'More than Princess Diana dying?'

'I'm not sure there's any point ranking it like this, but there may be some humans whose death would upset me more than Ubac's, or than Ïko's did.'

'That's nuts . . .'

'Please don't make me give you a list.'

'Well, *I* prefer people!'

'But you can love both. Love is generous enough to agree to being shared, isn't that what they teach in church?'

'That's ridiculous.'

My mum wilts visibly, Jean-Pierre splutters, my brother decides it's the perfect moment to slice some bread and Ubac, proving less than usually aware of the need for a truce, swallows loudly in reaction to the arrival of the gravy. We're all set to say grace.

'Actually, hang on, how come you get to classify love? Why should my love for Ubac be contemptible while the love between Jean-Paul Sartre and Simone de Beauvoir is so noble?'

'Maybe because it's reciprocated!'

'Loving him's enough for me. Because you see, I'll never know if he loves me, ever. And loving with no guarantee that you're loved back . . . I wonder whether that's the definition of true love.'

It's a shame, Christmas got off to a good start; I've even brought someone with me which is what they've been asking for since last century.

# 11

# A new home

Ubac and I were very soon made homeless.

My landlords had no legal right to do it, but this wasn't about the law, it was above that, a question of graciousness. They imparted the information with mincing words and stiff formality, thinking this would be enough to validate their case.

We went from one holiday let to another, slept in the van a lot, the two of us on a snuggly mattress, then on one serendipitous day's wandering, we reached the promised land of Le Revoiret, a hamlet hidden on the banks of the Rhone, near Belley. Everything there is black or grey, and asleep, life goes on in a wash drawing of India ink. The old bread oven, which stands surrounded by six houses, still has soot from bygone days of a communal life.

Jacqueline and André, their voices mellowed by their rugged existence, let out a little tail end of the house attached to their home, not so much to supplement their post-retirement income as to liven the place up.

The winter may come whistling through the windows, but the rustic character is calming, there's nothing here that doesn't serve a purpose, nothing that's been allowed to accumulate other than books. André has given me access to his bookshelves which are teaming with thousands of stories similar to the ones he likes to regale me with over a coffee or ten-year-old Ardbeg when Jacqueline's running errands in the village. André can help a cow to calve, cut purlins for his roof and recite Baudelaire – were the days longer in the past? Some evenings I hear a knock on the shutter and on my doorstep I find steaming soup that's turned up on its own along with a slice of rye bread. Well, when there's enough for two . . .

The semi-detached houses are surrounded by huge grounds that we share just as we do a love of animals. In their house there's Tchoumi, their jet-black Labrador, a proud, ageless dog who makes sure her owners' lives still have some spark. She's well fed and doesn't take much exercise – a body like a cocktail sausage with four cocktail sticks for legs would pretty much be the photofit for this friendly old girl. André has an unusual relationship with animals: he likes them, they discuss the fact between themselves and very much return the compliment. If a cat has the choice between ten laps, it will end up on André's and a ladybird will always choose his shoulder.

I like Le Revoiret as it's on the very fringes of the

world, you leave the place, you come back, nothing's really the same as anywhere else; André, who likes old words, says that in these mountainous parts, it's best not to be afraid of the local vernacular. Or of closed shutters. The prevailing mood is polite kindness, a feeling from times past. Everything here takes its own sweet time, to the point of interrupting its progress. This place was waiting for us and although all too often wreathed in thick fog, it suits us better than glittering lakesides. There's a hill behind the house that they walk up and back down at the end of every afternoon, and Jacqueline calls it the *mountain*, and she's right – it is one.

Louisette is the hamlet's other inhabitant. She lives opposite, alone, in one of those ancient houses with small windows that are always lit up. Her old-fashioned name gives an indication of her age. Despite her weakness for buttery sauces and rum babas, she's very slight; there seems to be an age at which the body makes a definitive choice about its disposition. I really like Louisette too; in her quavering voice she talks engagingly about life and the accommodations we must make with it. She complains about all the things that get difficult with old age – macular degeneration, how Vichy pastilles have doubled in price, her feckless nephews, the way the seasons are dying – and grammar too, then concludes that we mustn't complain. Whenever she sees me, she comes up with any excuse – three logs that need taking inside, a light bulb to screw in – and asks me to drop by. There are two cloudy bottles of Saint-Louis permanently on the table, and she pours it generously with a shaking hand. The cellar's full of it, she tells me, might as well do it justice while she's alive. At her age, prevention no longer seems to be an issue. Ubac, on the other hand, doesn't really like her, he yelps constantly and never lets her stroke him, he must have the key to mysteries I can't even glimpse.

When I go to work in the morning, I leave him in the grounds and all his distress pools in his eyes which he exploits with admirable skill. If I forget something and pop back barely five minutes later, Ubac is already nowhere to be seen outside. He's put his paws on the Carrels' kitchen window, done whatever it takes to catch André's attention, persuade him to let him in and get on with their breakfast together. Bits of *biscotte* accidentally fall from the walnut-wood table and end up in one dog's mouth, then the other's. Jacqueline mentions Tchoumi's diabetes, grumbling, and André pretends to concede the point. This heart-warming scene plays out every morning and I thank providence.

During the day Tchoumi teaches Ubac all the knacks for opening doors, clearly expressing his requests and securing satisfaction. She's the feminine presence he was missing and is emboldening him, just the right balance of maternal and cunning. In exchange, Ubac comes over all macho, thinking he terrifies every passer-by who has the cheek to come into the grounds. Wherever he is in life – whether it's for two hours or two years – he will assert himself as the rightful tenant; the domestication of dogs doesn't appear to have snuffed out their proprietorial instinct or perhaps we've projected ours on to them because although we pee less, we put up a lot of fences. I can quote Rousseau to him as much as I like, convinced that all our woes date back to the first person who fenced off a plot of land and dared to say, 'This is mine,' but he couldn't care less and goes straight back to guarding his territory. When the cheeky passer-by is a friend of the Carrels' and André opens the gate for them, Ubac greets them as a friend, thrilled to see them. When I return from the school at the end of the afternoon, I meet Jacqueline and André on their way back from their mountain, holding hands and with one dog on either side of their tender pairing.

In the evenings, Ubac sits quietly beside me, and I knead his thick coat with one hand until he hears the door. He then leaves me unceremoniously – dogs have a remarkable ability to enjoy any amount of stroking and then walk away from it without a thank-you or a bow or even a glance. They probably know that the petting is equally rewarding for the giver . . . or that our obsession with acknowledgement is ridiculous. Anyway, the noise at the door is André indicating that it's time to go and shut away the chickens at the top of the village, as he calls it. For this nightly act of bravura, Ubac is rewarded with a large hunk of rind from a Dent du Chat Gruyère, which he gobbles down before getting back to me, anxious about a potential need to share it.

Every Wednesday the little beige truck that belongs to the butcher-cum-cheesemonger-cum-market gardener and dates back to the previous century cleaves the chill dawn, toots three times and parks in the middle of the hamlet. A door opens and the first two customers race over on their eight eager paws; gobs of ham fat drop to the ground and are swiftly despatched. These will be good years, equitable in every way, detrimental in none, but it's still too soon to know that.

When we lived at Bourget-du-Lac, Ubac's vet practised in Belley. Docteur Domenech had been recommended to me. At the first consultation, he asked Ubac, 'So, young man, what do you make of life?' as a perfect opening gambit. There's a highly developed tenderness about the man, a wisdom that various entanglements with happiness have built one step at a time. He told us that, sadly, he couldn't continue to care for Ubac because he was setting off on a lifetime's project: a round-the-world trip by boat. Giddy-making, he said. It suited me fine that his hunger for freedom was the thing bringing his continuing care to an end – people who live on the edge are sublime. I wished him a great trip and he recommended a colleague, Docteur Sanson in Chambéry, when we now lived in Belley . . . there's logic in everything.

This Mr Sanson is a very thin young man with veins all over his arms and lots of laughter lines around his eyes, the sort of person – and these are key criteria – you'd happily join for a beer and a trip to Vienne on skis. He gives the lofty peaks of his learning and his rarefied qualifications a good dusting of levity. Whatever the news is, life always wins the day. When I don't know whether I should say *anus* or *rectum* to describe the area that seems to be troubling my dog, he says *bum hole* and I understand him. He will one day teach me mouth-to-muzzle, a technique that could bring Ubac back to life.

The first trips to the vet are on the uphill slope. It's almost a pleasure to come along and hear that everything's fine. Ubac is weighed, examined, studied from every angle; he's growing, putting on weight, filling out, he's prodded firmly as any solid structure would be. There's regularly one part of him that's growing faster than the rest, creating an unflattering lopsidedness but it all eventually evens out. His first appointments are all life force, invincibility and happy outcomes. The subdivisions of a life are actually quite straightforward: a beginning when we grow and an end when we decline, and the whole precarious gamble is to devote the largest portion to the first act.

These appointments are all alike. Ubac comes into

the practice moderately excited – there are people, noises, and a good smell of dog food and his fellow creatures. Not one hair of him seems to grasp that pain could come meddling here. His toing and froing keeps setting off the doorbell and this makes everyone laugh – unintentional comedians are always the funniest. Lots of people tell him he's beautiful and he writhes appreciatively, apparently never wearying of it. A few customers gaze at him sadly. I give my name at the reception desk, never sure whether to say it's me or Ubac who has an appointment, and hand his well-kept health record to the likeable young woman at reception. All entrenched ideas inevitably limit their own scope, but I've never met an unfriendly veterinary assistant. Ubac is the practice favourite.

We're asked to wait and we sit in the dog zone; vets' practices are like parliament with two camps eyeing each other and systematically disagreeing (the opposition in this instance is the cats). Waiting here means leafing through a dog magazine you leafed through last time; watching a shopping channel on which a confident variation of Snoopy talks up the latest lifesaving molecule; opening the comments book and closing it again because the words are too tearful; reading the small ads – about matings, grooming and doggy day care – on the cork board; chatting with the human–pet pairing next to you about the animal's name, age and reason for their visit; and lastly, and most importantly, it means calling Ubac to heel because he keeps doing pre-diagnoses on every visitor in the room, even the cats in the opposite camp. Some are in their travelling crates: Ubac wonders why they're incarcerated and how long their sentence will be. Here, just like anywhere else, he loves everyone; here, rather more than anywhere else, he must sense a climate of anxiety, so as a creature of prophylactic care, he encourages everyone to feel okay. Is he so lovable because he gives so much love? Only boxers arouse any mistrust in him, for no other reason than their inexpressive faces. (But there's nothing boxer-like about Louisette.)

Then Docteur Sanson opens a door, you can never be sure which it will be, calls, 'Ubac!' and Ubac races over, surprised someone knows his name. The two of them seem pleased to see each other, they both have the admirable habit of granting their full attention to whomever they're with, and it's only afterwards that I'm greeted – a protocol I'm very happy with. Ubac will treat every vet, even the one who provokes squeals of pain and fans the flames of his memory, with the same sweetness devoid of any resentment. He can probably tell they all want to save his skin.

The lively little thing is put on the examination table, he'll soon be hopping up there himself. I hold his head and whisper a childish rhyme that only the two of us can hear while his vital signs are measured. They're all making good progress; nature works well. The vet looks at his teeth, eyes and legs as you would a thoroughbred's, he asks whether I've noticed anything unusual, should I mention the sloppy poos at about eleven in the morning on Thursday the sixth? A vaccination, a worm treatment or some other preventative measure and we're all done. Ubac is set back down on the floor.

The vet applies a sticker to his health record as if ratifying a promotion, scribbles a couple of words on a file, hampered in this by Ubac who nudges his elbow with his nose, glad the man didn't find anything alarming. I conscientiously plot his weight on the graph, which we'll do for the first six months, then abandon. Lastly, we pay a lot but without thinking about it, and say goodbye. Ubac comes out exhilarated with what he's seen and smelt, and because he's successfully ensured that his tomorrows will run smoothly. Does he already know that some day the story between these walls won't be such a happy one?

The early visits form a succession like this, set to the pace of non-existent fears and complete faith in the future. Were it not for the agonised eyes of men and women who dare not cry as they leave alone or burdened with a small cardboard box, were it not for the unambiguous yowls of other Ubacs, we could believe that life never goes downhill. For many years, it will be like this, vaccination reminders and the soon forgotten privilege of being in good health.

Ubac and I find ourselves in the Beaufortain valley more and more often.

Weekends, holidays and probably excessive periods of truancy. There are places that make you welcome like this, and you mustn't fight it. Nothing here offends the eye, everything speaks of balance, there's a sort of concordance between the people, the land and the pace of time. The mountains in this range are either rounded or steep; we visit these contrasts and, depending on the fluctuations of our life, seek out thrills or level calm. I find myself loving this place with an arrogance I don't like.

Chambéry is gradually drifting away, and we now have to add a more local vet to Docteur Sanson for emergencies and peace of mind. It will be the Four Valleys practice in Albertville – in this part of the world every business is named after a mountainside, a summit or the ibex. Four is also how many vets there are. Docteur Fourget is pretty much in charge by the looks of things, a man who talks as loudly as his heart is gentle. By contrast Docteur Wicky doesn't say anything, to the point that you find yourself wondering whether he even enjoys this profession he exercises so masterfully. Docteur Bibal only laughs in leap years and seems to see serious issues everywhere, but Ubac likes him. He will be replaced (for anyone hoping for a long robust life, witnessing a vet's retirement is a fairly promising sign) by Docteur Deleglise, a thoughtful young leading light whose soft steady voice alone goes some way to healing ills. Orchestrated around these four men is a team of female veterinary assistants who juggle everything from admin to concerned customers, from sales to surgical aide, all of them endowed with the grace of cheerful friendliness and the immeasurable nicety of remembering exactly who you are. One of these women will save one of my dogs' lives.

These varied individuals who become part of my life feel to me like a crew so indispensable that it's as if we chose them and will gladly travel down a river's capricious meanderings with them. At first, it's calm, smooth and glinting. Steering the raft is easy, hardly an eddy. It's all about living in the moment and enjoying ever-increasing pleasures, being lulled by the absolute conviction that it will be like this all through life and not worrying about what lies downstream – why would you when tomorrow's in good hands?

Of course, there's the occasional bump that buffets you but nothing serious, and all they do is confirm how sturdy the craft is: the mechanical pain of an active dog, after all dogs have muscles, tendons, bones and a mechanism not that unlike our own, right down to its stiffness thresholds. Nothing unusual but enough to ask the question. Bibal tells me not to wear my dog out too much; meanwhile Sanson assures me that with no other artifice than the actions of my own body, Ubac will never tire before I do, and I subscribe to this notion of his superior vigour. Sanson also says no one knows this dog better than me and the plan doesn't seem to be to wear him out – I really like the man. So we run, we jump, we slip, we get back up and fall over again. These minor bumps seem to strengthen Ubac rather than put him at risk; life continues with its prodigal supply of entertainments, and you can never trust it too much.

Then the river becomes more nuanced, treacherous. The flow is manageable, the banks bewitching but there are discreet shifts in the water which, if you overlook them, will pitch you overboard. Little things, so negligible you barely dare mention them to the vet for fear of looking like your dog's overanxious solicitor, but enough of a thing to remind you that there are vulnerabilities and uncertainties in this life. Ubac will succumb to the tick-borne disease piroplasmosis three times. It should kill him twice. The last time, he came within a few hours of it.

So, Ubac's attending peacefully to his life, eating, sleeping, playing, then he collapses with no warning, his urine's the colour of coffee, his eyes bulge with questions and he's tired of being alive. In some instances, time is the only healer, but now it's the first enemy. In the scant thirty-minute trip from Beaufort to Albertville, 1 keep turning round to check he hasn't died. At the practice Docteur Wicky knows from a few drops of blood on a slide: 'Piro!' Fire. Again. Third time around it kills, no one has three kidneys. Ubac stays there for two days, waiting for his vital signs to improve. Ticks are a plague to the whole world, an ugly, insidious and self-important needle of a head that sucks out all the life around it and kills even the most arrogant mustang: And piroplasmosis is an illness of shame because it highlights your failure to notice the ticks, but what to do when there are sixty of them sucking at your dog's body and you think you're out of trouble when you extract and crush the fifty-ninth? Don't try telling me every creature has a purpose on this earth: this particular one, swollen with other animals' blood, is only here to ruin lives. Only flies – who, once the ticks' job is done, clock in with their hideous voracity – can compete with ticks for the position of most despisable life form.

Another time, it's something even smaller. People with dogs in their lives worry about thirty-eight-tonne trucks but it's actually a few millimetres that do for them. Thanks to a slanting shaft of light, 1 spot a tiny growth in the corner of Ubac's eye – growth is just the word, it sounds so benign. Fourget does the officiating, he's the specialist when it comes to skin, that precious membrane that dogs hide with their fur. The annoying thing with him is that for every clinical symptom he plays a game of algorithms. He opens wide the door to his extensive knowledge and, taking this so-called growth as a starting point, lays out all the probable options from the most commonplace to the most dramatic word ending in *-oma* which arises in only three per cent of cases. Of course, aided and abetted in this by the requiem that is the internet, you end up thinking those three make up the full hundred, and fate sometimes proves people right in this predilection for worst-case scenarios.

Then the diagnosis narrows down and mutilates . . . the vet needs to cut open the forehead of a dog who never asked for any of this, make holes and lumps in him, extricate this minute thing, put it into a small receptacle, then into an envelope, then you have to post it off to a lab, possibly pray to gods you've always laughed at, and wait. Wait for the vet to call and pronounce long words that shorten lives, something like *mastocytoma* – common but sometimes a killer. To be safe, the vet concludes, you'll need to keep a close eye on Ubac. That was the plan anyway, but life's getting more fraught.

These shifts in the water are game changers, the journey becomes tense, you start looking out for torrents and appreciate the lulls less fully. The consultations have lost some of their nonchalance. I often have to help the vet hold my dog, so he doesn't wriggle too much, to avoid him being hurt, to move aside some part of his body, to observe. I feel appallingly guilty with a sickening sense that I'm the source of his pain, and only too aware of the fear inflicted on him. Ubac lying on his side with me pressing down on him in a lead apron; our eyes meet and I can see he doesn't understand how I can be complicit in this unequal battle.

Back at home, I have to hurt him again, bandage him, get him to take medication using all sorts of tricks, the most perverse of which is gentleness. He sometimes moves away when I come over to him, he's never done that and I'm frightened he'll stop trusting me. I come out with trite expressions – 'It's for your own good' when everything I'm doing looks bad – and I clutch at any convenient theory, including the one that he believes in the benefits of what I'm doing. This sparks a furious debate between a part of me begging to leave him in peace, let him have his fun swallowing bumblebees, and another part that's convinced these unfriendly interludes are necessary to ensure he has a long life. Intense or long-lasting – who hasn't considered life in those terms?

# 12

# Mathilde

'Where the hell's Ubac?'

On the rare occasions when he's not here beside me, this question comes up again and again. In the eyes of my little world, we form a dyad, a living organism, neither him nor me but made from both of us. I don't think I've ever spent so much time with a single living being. When I walk, we walk. When he stops, I stop. 'It's hard to tell who's leaning on who!' a passer-by said once when Ubac and I were lingering somewhere, knee to flank. Yes, there's a bit of that, a reciprocal balance, like the arch stones of a vaulted ceiling meeting to form a sturdy whole. And anyway, what's love unless it's no longer being alone?

I sometimes find myself not wanting any other relationships in life; it's worrying. Is there no room left for other kinds of warmth? There are my friends, my family, my team-mates and I'm not withdrawing from them, I spend time with them, elated that Ubac has become a part of these groups, taking a place that's all his own – somewhere near the centre – and filling it perfectly. But as for a more intimate connection, a close, sustained and unique relationship, something you'd call love – I don't think about that, not as much as its lack should warrant.

Mostly we're alone, 'both all alone', as a child might say, not fussed by the absence of logic. Going for walks, hugging, visiting friends, welcoming guests, drinking coffee on café terraces, hearing and passing on news, going away for weekends, heading out to see a view, having compatible interests, missing each other . . . the things you'd usually do with other people, that's what we do. If you have a dog, you're part of the world without being completely a part of it. You're not on the periphery, you're properly in the world, but gloriously translucent, as if you've given yourself permission to exist in an enjoyable, temporary and disguised solitude. If you're always on your own – sitting on a bench, walking through crowds, streets and forests – people worry about you or think you're misanthropic, but if you're with a dog, they leave you alone. Some people will understand, knowing that this exile affords far more comfort than the deprivations it's associated with. I get plenty of affection, life is generous in every way and, not that this will please self-styled psychologists, people don't necessarily get a dog because they're missing something – they're allowed to have more than one reason.

But much as I like the idea of a man and his dog being enough, I'm wary of backwash. I'm all too familiar with giving the impression of rejecting the world, the damaging effect of being cut off from it and the abysses to come; humanity doesn't really wait around for you to return to its favour, and you can hardly blame it, it's been shown often enough how little a man is worth. And there are other reservations. There's the fact that the attachment I have for my dog and that he returns to me produces a furious longing to give more love, pretty much all the time. There are my doubts about my own appeal without Ubac's overabundance of gorgeousness. And, despite the joys of sharing my life, there's a skulking urge to reclaim the power of an identity all my own.

A few female visitors have come and lost themselves by my side for an evening and a morning. Briefly. They thought Ubac was really sweet – whether they meant it or it was part of a charm offensive I've no idea. He couldn't understand why my bedroom door, very unusually, was closed and why we didn't play hide-and-seek after supper. Being so constant themselves, dogs can't conceive that humans fluctuate between registers. But he didn't make a big thing of it, despite these oversights and despite the bodies clutched closer together than usual. In his eyes these visitors were just more humans and, equipped with his gift for predictions, he must have known they were only passing through.

Sometimes, jerk that I am, I was glad we were left alone. Ubac and me.

But out in the world, in amongst the billions, there's Mathilde.

One cold Thursday in November, as I came out of the Astrée 13 Amphitheatre in Villeurbanne, numbed by an incomprehensible psychophysiology class about reflexes and unconscious gestures, our eyes met, stared, almost challenged each other. It was 10.20 in the morning, there was a smell of cigarettes and coffee . . . if the class hadn't been starting again, we'd be there still. We'd never noticed each other before that day, maybe we hadn't existed. She's a brunette, with dark hair, dark skin, and dark eyes that tell you to move along. White erupts when she laughs and, because she's very receptive to joy, that happens a lot. In a tracksuit, the official uniform here, she's elegant – a gift not granted to everyone. She is often exuberantly self-confident, something people do when they're eminently unsure of themselves. Each monitoring the other's routines, we met again rather less by chance, and then thanks to chance, which determines everything, it turned out that a few university mates were, as well as being a good laugh, mutual friends.

Then came the coffee machines, the banter during breaks, the serendipitous grouping in practical classes, the excuse of revising together, the other person's company sought out, necessary and prodigious, the way the body moves seeing as that's what Sport Science is all about, the Thursday celebrations, the convenience stores and betting shops, and the nights spent putting the world to rights and extricating ourselves from our respective lives for the time it took to imagine the contours of a new life, one step at a time.

Our lives were actually very similar, their trajectories, their rebounds, their defensive walls. It was as if we were on the same route and, even though that presaged a match, it's always tougher getting parallel paths to come together. It was an enchanting dance, a dance to be prompted then delayed, never hurried, listening out for its invitations but agreeing to think in months and years, distensions of time necessitated by respect for the other person and the presumption that this would be special. Because from the very first moment, there was a sort of hovering conviction that some day our lives would be connected but this was hampered by our loyalties to others to whom we'd made big promises, and we hoped that the inescapable facts would ease them away as graciously as possible. There was also probably a lurking fear – classic during the preliminary stages – that having access to reality would kill the dream and the arrogant belief that there was more to us than a housing savings scheme and some IKEA wardrobes.

I think Mathilde is beautiful, and she and I share a vision of the world, with just enough differences to add us together. When we see each other, we start a sentence the day before and finish it the day after; at night over glasses of wine, conversations become heated but not excessively – if they catch fire, it won't be a wildfire. We sleep in the same bed, wanting only to watch over each other, and that sometimes intertwines us. She's the sister I was missing, and you think twice about fancying your sister. We talk about everything, say a lot about what the other has inspired in us and how they've enriched us. We admit our failings and both pretend not to have noticed each other's. In the bars and brasseries we head out to whenever we have the time, we watch couples who have nothing left to say to each other until their food's arrived, we snigger awkwardly, sure of what we are. From oak flooring to Levi's 501s, everything is more beautiful when it's old and worn. Not love. Together our life is powerful, and a part of me whispers that this intensity will easily stay the course.

We also talk about dogs, she tells me about her childhood spent on all fours, her hair wet and stuck to her face from being licked by dogs – Taquin, Wapiti, Tupoleff – that belonged to uncles and aunts, always other people, and Bernard's Citroën BX which reeked of Rako. Mathilde loves them. Otherwise, I don't think I could see myself loving her. Otherwise, we would actually never have brought our lives any closer than the odd happy hour because you can spot whether or not someone loves animals straight away – something they do or don't say or do – and, along with their other likes and dislikes, this makes up who they are deep down and determines whether you're compatible.

During a phone call Mathilde has said she'd like to come to Le Bourget for a weekend, if only to see this famous dog we spend whole calls talking about. Going to pick her up in Lyon (she teaches in Paris) with Ubac in the van is a moment of rare euphoria. That's down to seeing her again but also introducing them for the first time when – if the story's true – they'll have a thousand sunrises together. We greet each other with a big hug – a peck on each cheek wouldn't make any sense – and I quickly open the van's side door. Ubac leaps out. Pride is a ridiculous emotion but that's what I feel. Mathilde has her first sight of him: she's stunned as if she's just been given what she's been asking for since her first letter to Father Christmas. There's some paw-shaking and hugging and some little whoops. Then they do a lot of running around and jumping about at a nearby football ground. They couldn't give a stuff about me, it's perfect. This is their meeting, I'm the dumbstruck spectator, and of the four billion beats that I hope will pump through my heart, these particular ones have now been archived.

That evening, sitting at my tiny wooden table which has the advantage of bringing people closer together, we pick up our conversation that was interrupted two or three months ago. It's about the things that make life arduous or more wonderful, or something like that. Also news of Romain, Sylvain and a few other mutual friends. Having Ubac around is very useful, leaving less room for awkwardness and filling the increasingly intrusive silences; however much we tell ourselves we have our whole lives ahead of us, desire has a way of firmly shaking certain sand timers. Ubac here, Ubac there, a helpful diversion which allows us to dodge any final declarations, those last few steps when, whatever cup you're about to sip from, neither of you is daring enough to voice the truth. Meanwhile, that truth pounds so loudly inside that you think it must be audible, but it still needs to be put into words, a few letters, a gesture, a few centimetres for it to burst into reality. Ubac doesn't object to playing the starring role and we're still at the stage of talking about beating hearts and gazing eyes, so that's fine. I hope life spares me from spending a single day with this woman when all I want is to remember to buy the right brand of yoghurt.

Mathilde and Ubac play together, performing tremendous conjuring tricks inside and chasing each other outside in the garden – now, those are two generous hearts. It goes on more or less all night, and the few times when Mathilde and I find ourselves quietly side by side, nothing is conceded. I watch them, they go well together, I'm seeing what I wanted to see. They have the same energy, the same thirst to seize the moment, the same happy focus on each other and the same who-gives-a-damn-how-much-noise-we're-making.

What does a dog do when it laughs out loud? Ubac's tongue is lolling out and he's steaming up the whole world, Mathilde has scratches on both cheeks, it's not a girly look, which suits her fine. I love the fact that she doesn't talk to him as if he were a three-year-old child – not infantilising shows respect. Ubac, meanwhile, is slightly different. More boisterous, more powerful, more male, chewing and mauling, then wimpish the next minute, taking refuge between my legs but still standing his ground. Is he changing because of his age or because there's someone else here? He seems to want to say, you're welcome here, please stay with us, but also seems worried she'll appropriate too much of his life. This dog who senses outcomes long before they're hatched must have realised that we, all three of us, are standing at a turning point in our lives.

They fell asleep in the early hours, finally tired of playing. Mathilde's head is resting on the black beanbag, the rest of her body is on the carpet – one of those short nights without a proper bed that are all remembered individually. Ubac has gone to the beanbag and carpet too, one front paw resting on his visitor's arm, his dewclaw prodding into it as if to say, don't move. I make some coffee, filtering it through kitchen roll, making a strong brew, very strong (our stomachs can have a rest on Monday). I study the two sleepers and think to myself that every morning could be like this: no love cancels out another, it's exactly the opposite. And if Mathilde and I tread the same path for a while into infinity, then someone other than me will know Ubac and be able to tell the world about the dog he was. She's the only witness I can think of.

The evening after that particular morning we made love and it didn't ruin anything.

# 13

# A fixer-upper

In the early months we see each other only at weekends and during the holidays; the Ministry of Education doesn't trouble itself with people's need to be together. Perhaps it's a good thing that this need is being put to the test? That year, the respective zones of France in which we live, A and C – that's just the way tourism sausages up the country – have only one week's holiday in common.

Mathilde's arrival in Le Revoiret in her red Peugeot 306 Equinox is always greeted with explosive celebrations from Ubac. Standing on their doorstep, Jacqueline and André welcome her with less jumping about but equal warmth; they know better than most how well life works as a couple. Tchoumi comes to see what's going on and gives a Labradorish sort of ululation that appears to express pleasure. André calls Mathilde 'my girl' and takes her in his arms; his own daughter, who's withdrawn to live with the nuns at St Cecilia's Abbey, is no longer around to be hugged. Ubac jumps, runs, turns circles and yips for joy at being reunited with his attentive friend Mathilde, then sits down between us, and we each stroke him with one hand as our periodically interrupted but dazzling life as a trio gently establishes itself.

If Ubac seems pleased with the turn of events, he doesn't forget to express his preference for exclusivity, blatantly backsliding into regressive behaviour: relieving himself inside, usually on the threshold of our bedroom door in the early hours; demonstrating an absolute passion for eating poo; resolutely chewing through some climbing ropes; scratching the plasterboard back to the studs; and other charming acts of jealousy intended to remind us of his rightful place and his fear that it might be somehow dissolved in the trio. Before signing up to complete loyalty and unswerving devotion, a dog can display – on the same day and to the same person – that it loves being with them but wouldn't be distraught if they could just clear off.

In the early days of this relationship, the sheer longing in our bodies means we make love with no warning in places that are accessible to Ubac's curiosity; these couplings would be less intense if we had to plan them or interrupt them to tell a Bernese Mountain Dog to go and find something else to investigate while we're at it. It's quite disturbing, irritating even, to feel a dog's rasping tongue on the soles of your feet when you're in the passionately focused throes of lovemaking, but that's what you get in a life with no schedule or barriers: everything gets jumbled up with varying degrees of harmony and decorum. Even though the roguish Docteur Sanson told me that only the dominant canines in a pack perform sexual acts publicly, I've asked André for the key to the door between the garage and the garden so that, every now and then, I can be sure that the only mating dance Ubac can focus his attention on is between the frogs in the yard.

At the end of the year Mathilde is transferred to the South, in zone B, which is no better, still four hundred kilometres from our semblance of a base camp but in a different direction, and with different hours to those adopted by our budding new existence. The administrative system is clearly making a point of assessing how determined our relationship is. Sometimes, at the end of the weekend, Mathilde may not dare ask me, but I can feel her need to drive off into this arid landscape with Ubac, as if wanting to take a piece of us with her and cheer up her workdays. Ubac hops into the back of the 306 without a second thought, and the way he takes life as it comes is the sweetest of remedies. In his big generous heart the deed is done, Mathilde is on a par with me. With the rear seats put down and his great head touching the ceiling light, he turns around and looks at me to tell me they're leaving and I'm not to worry. I wave till they're out of sight, around the corner by the chickens.

Then André, who's been discreetly leaving us to ourselves, opens the door a little and says, 'You come in, Cédric.' As he swirls his glass he explains what 'legs' or 'tears' in a glass of wine are, what they say about its value, and how a bottle of Machuraz can provide solace with many problems. It's Sunday. Monday and Tuesday are for remembering, looking back in the wake of the weekend; Thursday and Friday are for anticipation; Wednesday lasts longer than it should. Ubac, she tells me on the phone, prefers the mountains to the sea which makes life so flat.

Then the separation becomes unbearable. Not one minute long-distance – that's basically the plan.

Happiness is designed in such a way that it advises its adherents to sacrifice everything that doesn't directly serve it. Careers come to mind first for execution, we'll find better things to do with our lives than climb up through pay grades. Mathilde baulks at the institution that's using all its administrative decisions to thwart our fairly simple notion of happiness. She packs her bags and joins me in this place outside the boundaries of a clearly delineated life.

There's an age at which we believe we can twist the world until it gives in and accommodates our needs and turbulent enthusiasms, and the objective in life is to ensure that this expectation, confronted by wisdom, is extinguished as late as possible. Mathilde and I maintain this illusion as best we can, a coxless pair navigating between naivety and conviction. She joins me and we live full-time in André and Jacqueline's annexe, a wonderful period when we never lose sight of each other and the only dark clouds are the demands of office B124 at the local education authority where Mademoiselle Kill-Joy outlines all the sanctions incurred, the drop in income, the hike in disapproval. Admin is an engine with two speeds: slow when indebted to you and very quick to scold. This ignominy brings us even closer, and the pleasure of being together wipes away everything else.

Perhaps to further challenge the straight and narrow path and even though nothing around us is stable, we buy an old chalet in the alpine pastureland of Le Châtelet, lost in the forests and meadows of the Beaufortain, a long way from everything, including work. It has no water or electricity, the cladding is wormeaten, it's overrun by brambles and the whole structure is rickety but it faces due south, is surrounded by foxes and stags, and sits under skies where very vocal buzzards fly – features that not one of the three of us considers to be secondary.

When two people are merging their lives, there's a strong yet delicious tendency to withdraw from the world, and a perfect accompaniment to this is the isolating ally that is nature. Both our families are alarmed by our apparently random decisions but we're grown-ups; there are mutterings that, at thirty, we're behaving like teenagers which is good news – if every part of our lives is behind schedule, then death's sure to do the same. That's a classic of lovers' psychology at its most ardent: fanning the flames of lunacy with lunacy, deliberately defying norms and expectations in order to attract disapproval. Yes, we've caused the disapproval, but we don't admit this to ourselves, and try to treat it with regal contempt. Everything appears to thwart our dreams, and this does two things: it fuels our belief that the whole world is neglecting us; and it reinforces our conviction that, on the deepest level, we ourselves are all we need. This strategy can probably go so far that the chaos of life and the constant battle break down the kernel of the relationship more than they strengthen it. We'll keep a watchful eye out for the tipping point.

The three of us spend as much time together as possible.

During the week I work the hours that I have to. Mathilde and Ubac explore the woods around Le Châtelet and, come evening, they take me to see their finds: waterfalls, chanterelle mushrooms or deer in a clearing. Mathilde gets more and more admonishments; these woods are a sort of hiding place for her. I'm exhausting myself with the driving but I don't care, getting back to our little fort takes precedence over everything else. The days are all alike, but nothing's put

off till tomorrow, we walk hand in hand, Ubac sidles
between us, nudging our ten tightly linked fingers with
his muddy nose; we couldn't ask any more of life than
this photo-story.

We don't know it at the time, and that's just as well,
but these rebellious days will be some of the best. At the
weekend we head into the mountains to go climbing,
choosing routes where Ubac can wait happily for us
at the bottom, to the surprise and delight of other
climbers. At the Tête de Balme one day he even climbs
the first two pitches of 4b, then waits for us on a high
ledge, tucked into the rockface and sheltered from the
sun by a foil blanket. The next roped party will think
he's the yeti and be more startled than he is.

Winter's a good time too. Mathilde and I go skiing
in the morning, make love in the afternoon and eat
pasta and pesto in the evening. When we head out for
a few days with sealskins on our feet, Ubac comes with
us and we sleep in the tent. I tell him that all climbers
have to carry their own food, that's the rule, but I agree
to take care of his because he pays us back a hundred-
fold at night, heating the tent and warming our frozen
bodies better than the hot springs at Le Mônetier could.
He falls asleep in a matter of minutes, groaning con-
tentedly and snoring like a man. In the morning I can
tell from the look in Mathilde's eye that she strongly
suspects he and I were singing some sort of canon.
Ubac bounces out of the frost-covered tent as eagerly

as we would go to the beach; we just open the awning for him, and he darts out into the crisp air. We watch admiringly: in this harsh place he just needs to be himself and he can set off while we take hours of preparation and layers of goose down to survive. What's he made of?

On other days we devote our free time to renovating the chalet (a job – it goes without saying – whose scale we hadn't gauged), tackling it with our flimsy competence and scant savings. Ubac falls asleep fifty centimetres from the pneumatic drill and where walls with no foundations are collapsing; he covers his black coat with white plaster or linseed oil; he unearths decades-old objects, including a detonator; and befriends a couple of badgers, determined as ever not to encumber his life with mistrust for anything. In the evenings, armed with a camping stove and headlamps, we have dandelion soup followed by vanilla ice-cream coated in chocolate to ensure that our love of food continues on into the night. If it's still cold in the chalet which is open to the four winds, we drink wine. Life is wonderful and the only thing we need to toast our happiness is being together. Then we'll fix some windows where the gaps are, then some light that isn't candles, then a stove and hot water will come along and the fact that these comforts come incrementally will allow us to savour each one as the boon of the century.

Ubac is invariably with us. Wherever we go, he's there; his presence is obvious yet discreet, self-effacing. This big animal blends so effortlessly between doorways, table legs and the legs of anonymous strangers that we forget he's there . . . perhaps he knows, and this is his trump card to ensure we take him. And when we stop at a restaurant, a station or a meadow, he always uses one of two anchoring techniques: either he puts some part of his body on our feet, having grasped that any movement will start there, or, after a quick appraisal of the location, he'll settle himself at the crossroads of any potential escape. In either case he looks perfectly calm lying down with his head on the ground, but he has one eye on everything and one on us.

Raising Ubac in a way that we see as fair and harmonious could make us feel confident about having a child. A real one who talks, goes to school and would wish us happy birthday. But we don't want children, neither of us does; how often we've discussed it, happy that on this point too we have the same vision of life. No need to prolong our love by creating a new person, it will be strong enough to last on its own.

The dog is neither a substitute nor a projection. Ubac is growing up, growing older; according to the conversion rate, he's now older than we are. If he'd been our son, he would now be our brother and then tomorrow our father, in an inversion that proves how absurd it is to think of him like that. And as a living entity in his own right, Ubac bypasses any such confusion. Schopenhauer made his dog Atma his sole heir. It may seem a nice idea, but I think it does a disservice to both men and dogs; humanising doesn't produce lots of mini humans.

Neither do we think of him as a male with a gender-coded blue collar and a need to bulk up his muscles; he has his own life and he can do with it what he likes. In the natural world, away from impermeable gender stereotypes, females bite as well as nurture, and there are males that incubate their young. Still, it's not as if Ubac doesn't have an identity: filled with his personality and experiences, he'd be recognisable among millions. Together, we're a couple plus a sort of alter ego, right there, alongside us and part of us. Together, we're three living creatures, the end.

One day we were eating chocolates in foil wrappers, and each one had a different number on it with a pop philosophical explanation for the number's symbolism. We laughed at this nonsense . . . right up until the number three shut us up. That silvery paper showed us a perfect balance and the passage of time: yesterday, today, tomorrow. It seemed to be speaking to us. Two hard-bitten atheists and now the trinity was talking to us.

If people call us a family, we prefer *pack* because in a pack there aren't necessarily blood ties and the members don't need a ceremony to swear loyalty, support and freedom to one another. This little linguistic nod also means we can lend our lives some of the wildness they so sorely lack. And if some zoologist really insisted on identifying the alpha figure in this pack, well then we'd tell them it's our very genuine dream of eternity.

I was at the café des Sports in Arêches this morning and was served by the octogenarian manager Félicien – complete with his blue apron with one pocket, his spiral bound notepad, his biro behind one ear, and his 'that's four forty' whatever drinks you ordered. He served me my coffee with no sugar along with a bowl of water for Ubac – one of the pleasures of being a regular and feeling part of a place. He cradled his round wooden tray to his chest and looked around the room.

'Isn't your Mathilde here?'

And I knew that he wasn't just talking to me but to Ubac too, and was referring to an eight-legged configuration that, in his expert grandfatherly view, held together pretty well.

What a boost.

# 14

# Trips to the vet

There's another reason it's a good thing Mathilde is around.

We're going to the vet with more assiduous regularity, too much to suit our hopes for an untroubled life. Apparently, there are no long-term rights to happiness without paying a few ransoms.

None of the visits is blithely casual now. The way I used to picture vets navigating situations is becoming strained. What will they tell us this time?

A vulnerable Ubac doesn't wander about so much in the waiting room; he even ignores the other animals. He's just here, limpet-like between our legs, one window of time for Mathilde, the next for me, as if he's trying to hide inside us, he's even inching our chairs backwards. I no longer need to keep calling him back but rather to soothe him, his panting body and frantic memories as he begs us to leave and go back to our quiet life. This is fear cubed, his and ours. I wish we

were here for just a booster. The nonchalant appointments weren't all that long ago; it was yesterday and
we already wish we could be back there – brief lives
are no good at teaching you the agonies of time. Every
little anomaly is pointed out to the experts, nothing
runs smoothly now, everything leaps out at us, the
possibility of bad news plays a starring role and being
proved right for showing concern only fuels our future
concerns.

None of the vets tells us Ubac's growing anymore:
now he's ageing. Luckily, life has its fluctuations like
a river, and in between the fears there are the times
when things are better, when things are fine, until we
eventually forget and stop worrying. Fortunately, the
panics and our determined efforts to silence them are
surrounded by peaceful moments of happiness made all
the more sublime by a quality we now recognise only
too well: their transience.

At other times, our little family boat clatters into an
obstacle with no warning. It wouldn't take much for
the whole thing to capsize and be scattered by the
currents. Ubac is lying flat out on the terrace at Le
Châtelet. Usually, our morning reunions are full of
excess – the night resets a dog's heart to zero. I sit
down on the doorstep, and Ubac who so loves physical
contact doesn't come over. He wants to but his body

is paralysed. I go over to him, already sure something drastic is happening. I call to Mathilde. I barely touch him and he yowls. His eyes tell us he doesn't know what's going on and we're all he has, I do my best not to show him how frightened I am, and pick him up, trying not to hurt him. We climb twenty-six steps up to the car, I'm barely aware of his weight, the urgency excavating someone else's strength. The rotten wood of the last tread gives way, I almost drop him.

I need to drive fast but smoothly, call the duty vet on the way, it's Saturday. Once there, Docteur Wicky's calm manner does little to reassure us. After an X-ray and a scan, the diagnosis comes out of nowhere: a ruptured spleen, peritonitis, the beginnings of septi-caemia, imminent death. It's a question of minutes this time. A veterinary nurse has raced to work, and prep-arations are made for surgery. 'We'll call you this after-noon.' And there we are, alone and silent in the waiting room. Did we say goodbye to him properly?

Ubac won't appear again until two days later. In his cage. He's war-wounded, half his body shaved, stitches in various places, and maybe a hundred staples. We greet each other as if for the first time, he gives a plaint-ive whine, and I'm scared it will burst his belly. I don't want to cry but I cry a lot as a delayed reaction and because I thought the end had come. They're the same postponed tears shed in the name of all the world's pain. They hesitate for a moment, hovering briefly behind my nose, then give up the fight and flood the place – who classifies the reasons we suffer? Ubac licks my pain straight from my eyes, a taste of salt and love.

We can pick him up in two days . . . would they say yes if we asked to sleep here? We've naively brought him some black pudding to make up for the blood loss. He struggles to get up but is doing a little better, the light in his eyes is back, like the sun around the edges of a cloud, it's not beaming yet but things are already warming up. So now we know it can come to an end in a trice on a clear spring morning just like any other. We know this but forget it. If no one had been at the chalet that morning, he'd be dead. If we'd woken an hour later, he'd be dead. If Wicky hadn't spotted it, he'd be dead. It takes a lot to live.

Of course, his emergencies happen on bank holidays and at weekends, when you pay twice as much, but who cares. The subject of money has no business here, there will always be enough frivolities we can forgo. It's touching to watch pet owners who aren't all born into financial security, how ready they are to devote a large proportion of a meagre savings pot to their dogs, cats, donkeys and other ridiculous pets, depriving them-selves of flatscreen televisions, weekends in Majorca and things that would be non-negotiable for other people. During the 2008 financial crisis, a good many astute analysts predicted that Fido and Felix would, like all hobbies, be sacrificed on the altar of choices. It didn't happen, the money stayed where it was because the most essential hobby is loving another living creature – it comes at great cost and is also priceless.

Docteur Wicky saved Ubac's life. On another occasion, with Ubac's daughter, it will be Docteur Fourget, the operation of his career, he will tell us, hours spent untangling a recalcitrant floor cloth from her intestines.

Vets are superior beings. I'm not saying that sycophantically for fate to look on us favourably, it's too late for that. It's just the truth.

They operate on a cruciate ligament at eight in the morning, then an intestinal tumour at nine, help with a whelping at ten, identify an undetectable parasite at eleven, treat a glaucoma at twelve and somewhere in between save a crash victim with legs at right angles, howling with pain and dripping with blood. The afternoon will be similar in that it will be nothing like the morning or the next day. They specialise in everything, each undertaking what a fleet of ten doctors would struggle to accomplish, and all when their patients are incapable of telling them where it hurts.

They exercise their dazzling competence amid a charming mayhem that mews, barks, stinks, yowls, cries and never says thank you. At the end of the day, they say goodbye to their assistants, climb into their cars – which are not big, not black and not parked in a space reserved for Professor Thingummy – and go back to a home that's as far out in the countryside as possible. The next day, there will be more non-speaking patients for them and once again they will have to activate their humble and diverse curiosities, a process that looks very like intelligence itself.

We sometimes venerate them as saviours, whether it's for Ubac or another animal, and we sometimes despise them with their ominous narratives and their small margins of error – they come into our lives in this schizophrenic form. We often wish they'd tell us something different when their knowledge of dogs in general collides with what we know of our own specifically. I may not be an expert on anything, but I do know all about our life. Occasionally I'll cheat by not telling them everything, and I think this will steer their diagnosis and life in general, but they soon spot the ploy and I feel a fool for trying to lead them off course. But they infuriate me when they assure us that dogs don't feel this and don't think that, that they can't see red, pink and orange, that a Husky's happy when it's exhausted and its master's still yelling at it. How do they know? Have they ever been a dog, even just once?

Over the years we establish this strange relationship with vets until we readily call them 'ours', a connection that's all the more blurred because there's a whole choreography of interpretation to it. The most implicated individual still doesn't breathe a word, leaving the human that loves it at leisure to spot whatever signs suit them: a brighter eye, a less halting walk, a bowl of food accepted, a starry sky, evidence for the heart which, sooner or later, will have to be confronted with the rationality of a blood test or a scan, and it's down to the vet to take on the unenviable role of persuading you to accept bruising realities. There are times when the realities align with our prayers, and that's wonderful.

So these doctors in green come into our lives and, during the course of raptures and shocks, the inevitable, latent question of the end is raised. How far is too far? One day the river will stop for sure; no dog is immortal. He will have changed the world enough as it is. Captain Ubac and his crew will reach the sea, let's hope it's plain sailing, estuaries can be chaotic. The raft will now have before it a greater vastness than all of us put together, a glittering but dark expanse, and then it will be time for everyone to consider how appropriate it is to keep going. We humans ask ourselves this question that hovers between love and indecency, but with a dog it's so much more insistent, quick and inevitable. This makes us say whatever we want about the animal's last wishes and its definition of what's acceptable; and silence can be as distorting as it can be helpful.

I know that one day, whatever else we've managed to withstand, we'll be there, in a room off to one side that's a little darker than the others. Ubac, Docteur Fourget or another, Mathilde and myself asking ourselves this hellish question and having to decide – alone and with a syringe of pentobarbital to hand – what's worth living. Eventually, every raft sinks and its wood rots. We'll whisper to each other. Is this better than a violent death in full pursuit of a hare? If only I knew. Ubac must have an opinion.

But we don't need to think about that now! We brush it aside forcefully, full of faith in life, refusing to let it rear its head so soon. The dog's six years old, at what would turn out to be the midpoint of his life; he weighs a healthy forty-two kilos, there's not much tartar on his teeth, his bark reverberates around the valleys and he overlooks the whole world. We come out of the clinic. I brought Ubac in today to take fate by the neck and wring the life out of it. In the last few months when Mathilde has brought him on her own, she's come back with good news; when I've ended up doing it, the prognoses were less welcome. I wasn't going to entrust a life to superstition or burden Mathilde with responsibility for good outcomes. 'It's just a bad bout of gastroenteritis,' Fourget tells me. 'Ubac must have found some meat that was on the turn! Don't worry, it'll be over as quickly as it came on.' Fine by me.

And as we leave the clinic, Docteur Fourget comes with me and does something he never does because all the conversation here is about the animals' feelings. He says something like, 'You don't need to be embarrassed. Not when you're happy or frightened or sad. Waiting for someone to understand or accept your feelings is a waste of time and it's an insult to your relationship with Ubac. Don't stress about it!'

I say a slow thank-you and promise that I won't stress about differing views. I'm happy not to. Then I give him one of those end-of-consultation classics about, with the best will in the world, not wanting to see him soon.

And we laugh, convinced we've come up with a good way to feel okay about going too far and be happy with the lives we've chosen.

# 15

# Walks

I've tried it with *talk*, *fork* and *cork*. Never any reaction. However exciting I make the escapade sound, the homonyms don't have the same effect. Absolute stasis in my companion.

On the other hand, if I so much as whisper, 'Shall we go for a *walk*?' everything comes giddily to life. That's his word, the one that invokes all his enthusiasms. Constructed with twenty muscles, each in its rightful place and equipped to stand to attention, his ears prick up, or just one does on lazy days, and his eyes bulge incredulously. As if this was an unusual suggestion. His back end pops up like a spring, the front end stretches with a groan of approval and then he follows us all round the house, staying as close as he can, getting caught up in our legs, slaloming zealously and barking for fear we might forget the idea – he knows human promises are fickle. If this isn't enough, he goes to find his lead which we never use but what else could he choose to show us how keen he is? So we set things in motion; in fact, that's all the etymology of the word *emotion* is.

Over a million kilometres covered together, for sure. And if, inevitably, most of them are forgotten, I know that when the time comes to sell off my memories, the hours my dog and I spent wandering through nature will be the most lasting. Routes, trails, paths that we followed or carved out ourselves, dense forests, open meadows, riversides, wheatfields, circumferences of lakes, moss-clad hillsides, final summits, glaciers, parks, housing developments, scraps of nothing between vines or marshland, foul pigsties, dry ground, tall grass, dead leaves, rocky terrain, dust, scrub, snow, rain, heat, frost or warm foehn winds, sunrises, sunsets and darkness, a few minutes or several days. Everywhere except islands, and of course the mountains feature quite a bit. That makes for some unusual walks.

Whether we're running or strolling, Ubac is up front, always. To clear the way or warn of danger, to check that an abandoned crust of bread comes to him or so we can watch his back – he alone knows the point of going first. He turns round every ten metres, checking on us, then carries on. Once his course is more or less established, he zigzags (aha, so dogs are actually just like us, believing the treasure's always on the far bank). When he does this, bearing in mind he hates water, I tell him he's got a good tacking technique. The zone he explores is quite low: his nose rakes along the ground – I'm worried he'll bump into trees, but it never happens, even in the evening when the colours have faded. When he does look up, though, I like to think he's enthralled by the wide horizons. He waits for us at every intersection, whether it's real or symbolic; sometimes, to annoy him, Mathilde and I head off in a different direction, but he knows it doesn't make any sense. He gives a playful bark, and order is restored.

If I overtake him for a laugh, he starts trotting and eyes me reproachfully. If I keep going, he steps up to a canter and races ahead to bring my prank to an end without losing sight of me. Only on the occasional winter's day will he agree to go behind us; the humans might as well take the strain of plying through powder snow.

Wherever we are, we always have the same quest: finding somewhere to walk.

Sometimes it's obvious, there's green all around us, everywhere, at home and in life, and most of the time. But there are moments when we have to be wily, sniffing out a route, beating our own path, there's nothing but main roads, streets, car parks and roundabouts, airless and scalding hot brownish-grey ground covered in white lines – are these places called *landscapes*? When you live with an animal you become aware that the earth is divided into two zones: places where you can touch its flesh and those where it's been muzzled with asphalt.

In towns, those angular environments, we really have to search. We've become experts at finding parcels of vegetation, particularly Ubac. He can tell exactly where a city breathes and will take me there: improbable grassy hillocks nestled between two underground car parks, paths edged with bushes, a town hall's self-important gardens, a bed of stubborn hollyhocks pushing up the cobblestones on the Île de Ré like weeds, the vestiges of allotments coming into view on a street corner, or the flowers around an advertising billboard on which happy-looking people grow lettuces on their balcony. He follows invisible arrows that point him towards these breathing spaces, and even in the heart of a city the route to something organic seems strangely familiar to him. But more often than not we're lucky, our needs are met, there are great expanses, enough green to drown in, and imagination is our only limit. And then we all *go* for a walk, I attach importance to the phrasing, no one's *taking* anyone, there's parity in it.

Somewhere in the day, with varying degrees of planning, we will have this digression. A walk. A ramble, a trek, a hike (though none of these words captures the poetry of these outings). One hand held horizontally, tapping the other on the vertical plane: time out, downtime that appropriates life, suspending every other task. Ubac and me. Mathilde and Ubac. Ubac,

Mathilde and me. A guest. Even though this dog lives right in the middle of a forest and is free to go wherever he wants, we'll have this shared expedition. Always. On the old Chemin des Manons behind the chalet when we're short of time, in the Quatre Sous woods for an hour or two, through alpine peaks on days of complete freedom.

The idea's always the same: knowing where we're going but very happy to get lost, a sort of lucid aimlessness and we let our forerunner decide the way. What matters is less the available time than the pace of the walk: Ubac – and, I think, every other dog – doesn't understand when we rush the thing, because then what's the point? If it lasts only ten minutes because that's all the day's timings will allow, we have to give the impression it could last a lifetime. Ubac couldn't care less whether we go all the way to the end of the track at Le Pellaz where there's such a lovely view of the Pierra Menta; he doesn't care about going far, he's more interested in being out for a long time, and if we can't be, then we should at least go about it calmly. It's only at the very end that he changes gear. When we get home from a walk, I've hardly opened the door before he steams in, almost shaving off the sides of his head; all dogs, apart from real goody-goodies, do this, as if they're being pursued by a butcher with a meat cleaver.

What's really important is being together. On the few occasions when Ubac's somewhere else, being looked after by my parents or in some other luxury exile, it doesn't occur to Mathilde and me to go for nearly so many walks. As sporty endorphin addicts, we'll exercise, but just having a simple walk, putting one foot in front of the other, not so much. What's missing is the cheerful pretext of watching Ubac's comings and goings and his enjoyment of the outdoors. A dog's vocation is to protect us from inertia; it's an antidote to fossilisation. But beware because this business kills the elderly: when their dog dies, going out becomes pointless, joyless and hard work. Then, deprived of vitality and of their antifreeze, they in turn grind to a halt.

Ubac and I are walking along the ridge at Crête des Gittes. It's not very wide and it's hard to dismiss thoughts of the drop but he'll never fall. The panorama is understated yet spectacular as we look down on two lakes, Le Roselend and La Gittaz, and over towards a luminous Mont Blanc, and marmots are whistling harmonies in canon. Ever since he got his paws on one that was befuddled after five months of hibernation, Ubac has thought he can catch any marmot. They're not afraid of much, and even if one of these sleeping beauties were caught, it would, like the previous one, be immediately released by a Bernese Mountain Dog who still doesn't know what to do with violence.

There's more than the scenery to make you feel good. There's the unity of time, place, pleasure and action that really does the trick. When Ubac chews on a piece of wood, he seems happy in what he's doing, and the knock-on effect is that I'm happy too – not that I'd actually consider copying him. When I'm with friends, laughing loudly over a glass or several of Mercurey wine, Ubac takes pleasure in our guffaws, participating in his own way. So our joys are shared but they differ in their sources of inspiration and the rate at which they affect us. The same is often true with other people, we can be happy for someone else and through someone else, slightly in advance or just afterwards. But in this instance, when we're walking, our six or eight feet covering the same ground, these discrepancies are ironed out and I get the feeling that we simultaneously reach equivalent degrees of satisfaction – it's rare for happiness to play out in unison like this.

Even though driving rain forces his eyes closed, even though the wind makes his ears flap, even though he has a preliminary sniff at the sky's moods through a half-open door, Ubac doesn't really care much about the weather. Dogs don't bother about what it means: if it's raining, it's raining, end of story! Going out whatever the weather is by far the best idea. I on the other hand will look out of window a little anxiously, scrutinising, waiting for bright spells, plumping myself up with this or that fabric depending on the sky's potential mood swings and the lurking fear that it might slap me in the face. He waits for the door to open and steps out stripped of any doubt, from January through to December. You really need to have a special relationship with the outdoors to treat it with such constancy. He's made of different stuff, and I envy him his uncomplicated strength, his gentle resilience.

In the early days, I took an umbrella, it was pathetic. Then a state-of-the-art waterproof coat that was soon soaked, my damp shoulders hunching with cold as I prayed that Ubac would get fed up with the conditions and quickly decide to turn tail back to the woodburner. Nowadays I don't really mind that I'm not constantly surrounded by postcard blue: Ubac has taught me to savour the outdoors as it comes and to appreciate its extra character and aesthetic when it's turbulent because, like everything else, it's only ever what we make of it. If I had to choose one type of sky, I would tend toward the unsettled variety. It's a bit like life really: if it were permanently radiant or permanently leaden, that could get boring. We're at the mercy of its variations, and respect each of them.

Walking with a dog can teach us so much. Didn't Aristotle glean some of his ideas as he strolled around a grove? The very name of his Peripatetic School means 'school of walking'.

Firstly, I've learned that proximity and repetition can be sources of elation. I'm almost embarrassed when we head out – for the umpteenth time – to shuffle the dead leaves on the track below the house, the Three River's Point as we've called it, a path that schoolchildren used back in the century of walkers. He knows its every turn, the fallen beech tree before the stream, the carcass of a Manufrance bicycle at the foot of the bridge, the shrine overrun with thorns, twenty minutes on the way out, twice as long on the way back (that's what you get with mountain gradients), the familiar smells, sometimes a roe deer, the one with a dark leg. All that changes is the seasons, barely altering the colour palette.

I'd like him to run through Cirque de Gavarnie in the Pyrenees, along the salt flats at Mont Saint-Michel, do the whole *tra mare e monti*, surf and turf, but what's the point of the exceptional? It doesn't mean anything to him. Living's enough for him. The tiniest thing can make somewhere a destination or be an incident for him. Monotony doesn't sour life for him because it doesn't exist: Ubac has a gift for turning any routine – which in my demanding eyes is so tedious – into a pleasing experience that makes you more receptive. Repetition bores me but wins him over. It's quite something to see the everyday in such a good light, picking up on its small variations; it shows a gracious consideration for regular habits, and seems to make happiness more accessible. A tyrannical pursuit of novelty might deem this a diminished, unambitious approach, but Ubac is teaching me that ultimately it's the most subtle, and that doggedly trying to avoid banality is in fact the most fully realised expression of banality. Okay then, I'm up for the Three Rivers route again and again, for this pact with the transient nature of things, and for the great round dance of our life together!

Secondly, I'm learning that every moment warrants being lingered over. We've all pretty much had our fill of life coaches encouraging us to experience the present moment to its very core, to be guilt-ridden if we haven't done this in the past and to commit to doing it in the future, bragging about a timeless existence when all we actually talk about is time. The people painting this rosy picture often have grey complexions and their only success is that, at the end of the day, we like doing pretty much the opposite of what they're claiming to be beneficial. For Ubac the present moment is the only agenda, and he inspires this sort of attitude in me, and that's different. So a trip to Roche Plane doesn't mean getting bored on the last stretch of path through the blueberry bushes where you have such good views of the Albertville valley; nor does it mean looking back at where you've come from or eyeing up the Mont Mirantin which you'd quite like to go up tomorrow. It means being there, on that narrow stretch of path, with those three pebbles, that cloud and this confluence of seconds that deserve to be allocated a snippet of our messy lives. If we savour its every minute, life seems to stretch.

Usually, we need to catch a whiff of death before finally agreeing to notice the present moment, but this same magical behaviour can be inspired by a panting mutt: allowing the here and now to triumph effortlessly makes life radiant.

Thirdly, he's taught me that an aspect of the spice of life is uncertainty. When Ubac sees me pick up my grey trainers, he knows the chances of an outing together are going through the roof. If I reach for the green bag, he'll lie back down. And sulk a bit. In more neutral situations, I don't know what signs he picks up – a look, my behaviour, something invisible – but he'll know from the way I grab the keys to the truck and how I put my hand on the door handle whether he's coming with me. That's where his prescience stops. If he's involved in the trip, where are we going? To nearby Villard here in the mountains or Paimpol on the Brittany coast? For an hour or ten days? It doesn't much matter to him, he's instantly up for it and enthusiastic about it: dogs don't burden themselves with crystal ball gazing. Where else can you find an attitude like that?

Lots of friends and acquaintances want to know everything, right down to how they'll spend their free time, where they'll be in two weeks' time, what the view will be like, what other people have said about the tiramisu and the bedding, and what nasty surprises might blight the schedule. So basically, the plan is for nothing to happen. Ubac doesn't spend a single moment trying to minimise uncertainty; he doesn't have the means or, I'm convinced, the inclination. He doesn't expect anything and that seems to be a hellishly efficient way to ensure a lot happens. It's like travelling backwards on a train: you're not resigned or passive, wonderful things come along and you're never disappointed. And if my status as a human means – for whatever flimsy reason – that I can't throw myself body and soul into a life without a known trajectory, a life I can discover as I go along, then I still subscribe to the definition of adventure that Ubac has unwittingly given me. It has taught me to welcome the rich rewards of the unpredictable and, as far as possible, consent to being unaware of what lies ahead.

And there's something closely allied to not anticipating: not fearing. Wherever we go, whatever we plan to do, picking daffodils or jumping crevasses, Ubac has the same response: yes. He agrees, leaps to his feet and follows. His faith in me is spontaneous, complete and endlessly revived. So naturally, as newly elected presidents say, this faith is an honour and an obligation for me. Mostly, I think it's admirable because it's nothing to do with a lack of brainpower, lucidity or cortical architecture, or down to naivety or a tendency to neglect his own wishes in favour of mine (which some would describe as following blindly when he actually sees things as clearly as possible). No, it really is something extra, something lucid that's evaluated and then granted, a depth that I've never so much as glimpsed in a human being and that I myself lack even though I've witnessed it from front-row seats. A layer of intrepidness, that's the extra thing this dog has in his pericardium, an anomaly in his heart that radiates out to me. Because when you believe in another living thing that believes so completely in you, when a life so worthy of respect seems to respect you, then, in your amazement, you can start thinking of yourself as, well, worthwhile.

The day this bold heart decides its time is over, I can't think of any flesh-and-blood creature that will give me one hundredth of its vote of confidence or one thousandth of its enthusiasm. What I do know is it'll take a second miracle.

If we're alone on our walks, I talk to Ubac. A lot.

About hairline fractures in my heart and what repairs them; about how much compromising is acceptable, my absolute hunger for freedom and the intoxication of satisfying it; about morons and wonderful people; about my slightly shaky conviction that I've found my place; and about how he's doing. Nothing goes unsaid. Ubac knows everything about my life, the whole set-up, and I don't know how but he knows better than I do how I'm feeling. Talking to someone who doesn't reply – or so little that you end up baring your very soul – turns all this yomping over tree roots and patches of clover into therapy. If that means talking about yourself unselfconsciously, warts and all, well, then I'm happy to go for this method for wringing it out of me. It's true that in the places where we walk, surrounded by the calm of the outdoors, everything is conducive to being brutally honest about yourself, and there's nothing to hold you back, you can pour your heart out – it feels so good coming out and saying who you are. Then his throat produces a sort of grunt or gives a deep sigh, as if saying, 'We'll stop there for today.'

I'm always surprised, with a sort of joy intercut with anxiety, that this time spent walking freely, surrounded by silence and nature, still doesn't cost anything; some day the bitcoin world will register that these are the most valuable things. And so we walk along water-ways, in the rain if need be, happy together, extricating ourselves from our intricate life; and all its quibbling glides over us like water off a duck's back – we're more waterproof together. There's no more delectable way of baring my soul than when I'm in his company, and I still haven't decoded its magic: having him there helps me experience more fully a solitude that – I've discovered rather late in life – can be shared. There's nothing to do but walk and worry, at the very most, about the next step. Life is right there, so close by, but you whittle out the things weighing you down: the nosey neighbours, the work memo, and the cost of snow tyres.

I hope everyone can find these diverting geographies,

where you can regain control of untameable time, take your mind off things without speaking a word, find some answers to the wretched questions life keeps plaguing you with and, by some strange witchcraft, achieve a lasting effect where – once you're home – you glide through that life more lightly. Would it be the same if I were walking alone, without this dog who prunes away everything extraneous? To answer that question, I'd have to go back to that lone state.

After a while, out of deference to Ubac who has just as much right to tend to his inner world, I stop talking. What a relief. And that's when the walk takes on a second flavour: silent coexistence. What connects us to others better than silence? We humans don't like it much, we overlook the good it does, don't know how to handle it, it feels too final, we chatter to smother it. We may enjoy doing this, but like any pre-emptive safe-guarding measure, it's wearying in the long run. And the truth is there's no more precious company than silence. A dog will never resent you for not talking, it won't think you're bored or uncomfortable or that your relationship with them is breaking down; accept-ing that you don't need to say anything to each other is a unique pleasure. The day some crackpot researcher finds out how to get dogs to talk, Ubac and I will be long gone and that's just as well because unspoken thoughts will no longer have their rightful place. Here, walking silently beside the murmur of the pond at Marcôt in the mountains or amid the bustle of the Tête d'Or park in Lyon, a sort of gentle bubble, a dense yet light atmosphere screens us and allows us to daydream. And in this semi-conscious state, with not much on our minds, we achieve something like a mobile meditative state – with no incense and no invoice. Then Ubac barks at a blackbird and the bubble bursts.

Before we turn for home or come full circle we have a pause. It can last a while because doing nothing doesn't make dogs feel awkward either. We sit down, our heads on a level and, even though I firmly believe he couldn't care less about the view, we look towards the same horizon, which isn't a foregone conclusion in the mountains. I give him water, emptying it from my mouth into his, he splatters me with it, then licks my cheek which I really like even though I say yuck. A sunrise or sunset goes well at this point, Roche Parstire is perfect for it, you have to line up the sun exactly with a chiselled peak, and this thing you think of as fixed lurches away from the halo, rapidly appearing and disappearing, reminding you that life does the same. I say, 'Look how beautiful it is,' then remember how – as a child – I hated it when an adult trapped me in their aesthetic judgements, whether or not they were about horizons, and I shut up again. But I do feel it's never totally inappropriate to mention the power of beauty.

Before I stop talking once and for all, I turn to Ubac

and tell him he's my leveller – I like telling him that, my leveller. All our posturing and illusions provide us with a retreat that we alone are slow to notice and are at pains to recreate, but I can tell from the way he looks at me whether I'm on a level or listing, so having his incorruptible eye on me is a very valuable baseline.

When notions of the spirit and the sacred are unrelated to religion, we can experience powerful moments filled with worldly spirituality, moments that establish the only legible definition of secularism. Ubac waits politely and then, looking as if he completely understands, goes back to sniffing the trunks of spruce trees and to methodically marking his vast territory; I ask him why he doesn't pee out the whole lot in one go, his day would be easier than with these ridiculous little drainings, but he seems to prefer frequent stops. (It's only later when I go to a urologist to find out my brilliant PSA score and, with no warning, I'm required to 'tell me about your urinating', that I will stop hassling Ubac about this, probably also slightly envious of how strong his sphincter muscles are.)

Sometimes he stays beside me, his great head wedged on my shoulder, a rare boys-only moment, our own way of sticking one up to homophobes uncomfortable with any display of affection. His tenderness can prove self-interested: he's smelt the remains of a sandwich in one of my pockets. And then begins the umpteenth performance of the I'm-not-looking dance with the two of us sitting, our heads more or less at the same height: I take out the treasure and, staring straight ahead, start to eat it. I know I'm being watched so I stop chewing and look at him out of the corner of my eye; he then turns away casually, pretending to be interested in the subtleties of the sky, and as soon as I bring the sandwich back to my mouth, he starts watching me sideways again. We repeat this several times, I'm Laurel to his Hardy. I offer him a gherkin, he spits it out; a bit of bread, he accepts it; some Beaufort cheese, he's over the moon – he knows how to use his big eyes, the bugger. He wins me over and gets half the feast every time, but pretending he's not sure that he will adds a little something.

# 16

# Intuiting and noticing

One June night Ubac didn't want to sleep inside.

He never does this. He usually curls up in the hall, a perfect lookout post. But on that particular evening, it just wasn't happening. He lay down at the far end of the terrace, away from the walls, from the chestnut tree and from humans. I called him and he ignored me; I thought he must be too hot indoors. That night there were earth tremors that woke Mathilde and me. I glanced outside and Ubac was sleeping peacefully. '2.6 on the Richter scale,' ran the headline in the morning's *Le Dauphiné libéré*. It's a low reading but it was plenty from inside the house. Having had a close look at our talents as stonemasons, Ubac must have had doubts about the building's stability. Three years later, after hundreds more nights spent back in the hall, he re-enacted the scene, wanting to spend the night with only the stars as company. 'Gird your loins, guys,' Mathilde joked, 'we'll have an earthquake tonight!' The next day

*Le Dauphiné* reported a more impressive 3, and that a few hundred-year-old barns had collapsed. Ubac knew. So this dog with his cosy life was made of the same stuff as the elephants in Yala that anticipated and fled the tsunami. Who told him?

I like the idea of nature's superiority, its prodigious abilities that defy the authority of equations and of humans (an authority that's being undermined by progress), but much as I like it, I'm wary of lazily citing it in every instance. When Ubac's spleen ruptured, I loved the fact that we polluting city-builders had also invented mobile phones and scans, and that abominable chemicals stopped the bleeding – what difference would communing with the trees have made? And yet when we're surrounded by trees, Ubac senses things I can't. When I see him sprawled under the TV, it's easy to forget he's an animal and, as such, he's incontrovertibly connected to nature, he's a part of it, he *is* it. Like bears or weasels, he would never eat fly agaric mushrooms. Meanwhile we hyperconnected humans, in the biggest break-up story of all time, have lost our most beneficial connection and every walk I go on confirms this: soon the only birdsong our ears will register will be message notifications on our screens.

Ubac is re-teaching me to read the living world around me, to listen to nature's music, its amplitude and its pauses, to gauge its state and decipher its codes. Did I once know these things? Life has shown me that there's no more trusty way to get to know a landscape than by experiencing it bodily, at length, humbly and in all seasons, but Ubac is showing me something further: that you need to be a part of it, be one with it and not be afraid to let it permeate you.

There's no warning, he just suddenly stops. I don't know how he does it. He can tell, has a feeling, picks up some friendly but silent call that brings together invisible signs; I'm oblivious to any of this, but immediately after he stops, a vulture dives through the air, a swarm appears or the wind picks up, the world comes to life. And – always last to know – I'm stunned. One morning when we were on a short walk, Ubac led me away from the usual route, insisting on one which took me under the foliage of an oak tree surrounded by tall grass . . . that looked like any oak tree and any tall grass. But he stopped abruptly two metres short of a dip in the ground and gave me a meaningful look. In it was a day-old fawn; it was shaking and, to my human eyes, was clearly in danger. I called Georges, a friend in the forestry organisation ONF, who came to see it and said to leave it alone, everything was fine, definitely not to touch it and that its mother, who was probably busy decoying predators, would come back at nightfall. And that's what happened. Without Ubac and his sixth sense, that walk would have been just like the ones the day before and the next day; I wouldn't have learned anything about the language of the land and would have gone home none the wiser.

In the early days I thought his knowing and sensing things was chance, his discoveries were pot luck. But it happened too often. So I – who never sees anything coming and am as ill-equipped to be here as a stag in a city centre – have started watching and using his antennae: if his body language changes, if he stops what he's doing, I crouch down, concentrate . . . and notice something appearing in the distance, an ibex scurrying away or some other wonder that I would previously have missed. It's often an animal full of life force but on the lookout for danger, a magnificent anomaly; what is there to be afraid of here? I now occasionally spot things with him, at the exact same time and in the right direction, the ultimate reward which makes me want to relearn an aptitude for this place, for things my ancestors knew and that, through a series of distractions, we've lost.

Before having Ubac, I felt alone in the forests and mountains, and – having seen no one – I would brag about this solitude on my return. Alone in the world! He's taught me that actually thousands of creatures saw me, studied me and let me pass, and all sorts of scenes played out around me between the feathered, furred and leafed residents: diplomatic negotiations, battles, seductions, reunions, assemblies, lessons, ceremonies, guard duties, fears and joys,

births and massacres, ends and beginnings. I was indif-
ferent to these inhabited silences and Ubac gave me
keys to unlock parts of them, promoting me from a
thoughtless passer-by to someone who looks and sees.
He helps me read these stories, he speaks the language
and shows me how to go about enlivening what I once
reduced to a backdrop. You need only freeze, melt into
the background, awaken your senses and agree to be
receptive; it's so easy to be open that we've forgotten
how to do it.

Walking through the larches in Italy's Val Vény (and, on
reflection, Ubac doesn't speak a word of Italian) or the
rocky heights of the Bauges, Ubac sets out to connect
with the world. He listens, scrutinises, picks his way
through, climbs, digs, sniffs and gets scratched. He
engages fully with the substance of a place, its teeming
and meandering, he inhabits it. Through a series of
choices, we humans have favoured sight far above
the other senses and have thereby taken a backward
step. Our muzzles have been refined into little noses
that we'd prefer to hide; we're afraid of touching perfectly wholesome dust; we're quick to wash our anxious
hands; we pasteurise our tastes; we fill our heads with
noise and can no longer pick up soft rustling; but still
we humans enhance our eyelashes and have many more
metaphors about eyes than other parts of the body. This
decision may make our faces prettier but it's holding us

back from the world because sight has a weakness: it tolerates and maintains distance.

Ubac shows me how diving right in is in fact more subtle. His muddy snout, his dirty ears, the muscle spasms in his flanks tell him about mysteries, fear, death, mushroom rings. I can smell only a rose or animal droppings, can hear only silence or a racket, can see only what's visible. I'd so wish to have his grammar of nuances and I hope that the human love I feel for him and all the ways I help him don't diminish any of his abilities.

These walks are levellers, reminding me of my exact status as a living thing among others. That's honour enough. They bring me back to the land, the sky and the shy presence of trees; they add wildness to my life, dirty my hair, scratch my skin and tear my clothes. 'We're not brutes,' say the educated, the fashionistas. If only they knew.

Mathilde's mother, Doune, lives on the fourth floor of 29 rue Pionchon in Lyon. Ubac likes going there, a place where you can do pretty much anything, scuff the parquet floor, dust yourself with a cloud of flour and binge on pretzels. When he lets us know he needs some fresh air, we take the lift, press on the 'o' on the left-hand side and I fold over his tail before it gets caught in the door, then he skids across the faux marble in the hallway and we go out into the little Parc de la Ferrandière at the foot of the building. What we get there is car horns, a few plane trees with restricted crowns, some handkerchief trees, a bit of grass and a rectangle of wood shavings where dogs are supposed to relieve themselves, but they never set foot in it. This cooped-up slice of nature might seem small, cobbled together from leftovers and not worth noticing. Artificial, let's say it as it is. It would even be fine to laugh about it. Resisting as it does the onslaught of concrete along with all the indifference and din of the human race, it's actually as untamed as impenetrable scrubland or primordial forests – how stupid to talk about *right out in the country*, how stupid to classify.

We let Ubac wander in the park with his nose to the ground as he monitors the millions of abandoned smells. There was a time when I would have used this opportunity to make some phone calls, or I'd have taken one of Doune's magazines and leafed through it on a bench, occasionally casting a prefect's eye over his wanderings. I was only half there. In fact, all you need to do is be quiet, let silence take you over, focus your eyes on minute details and wait. You can also walk, taking soft footsteps that open you up to the park's secrets. And then things appear: a spider's strategy, the midges it's caught, the choreography of bees becoming besotted with city life, a sprinting mouse, ants in formation, a procession of caterpillars, flirting chaffinches, a gentrified hedgehog, swirling leaves and other depths inaccessible to hurried footsteps and blasé mentalities. Life, for those who want to see it, is everywhere, and anyone who says they're alone is blind. Ubac is teaching me the art of being attentive, spelling out the environment wherever he is, from breathtaking places that feature in posters to a little square you'd cross without noticing it. In his world view there's no exceptional expression of nature nor a cut-price version, there's nature in its diversity and multiplicity, and all of it warrants our engagement. Other than humankind's critical eye, nothing grants itself the right to classify nature's charms. Having been raised to believe there are a hundred must-see wonders, this is a major discovery for me: beauty is there for the taking everywhere.

As someone who braves storms and dizzying heights, who treads unconquered terrain, I talk a lot about nature and describe myself as at one with it. Ubac has put me right. Claiming to have a close relationship with nature isn't something you can earn with high altitudes at the Grandes Jorasses or miles of coastline at Cape Horn; there's the whole world and there are small details. And that's a good thing. The only preliminary work needed if you're to be receptive to these places and dare to say you're drawn in is to pay attention to them, from venerated edelweiss to modest daisies, from the strong *pampero* wind in Patagonia to the light *bisolet* in the Parc de la Ferrandière. But then I should have known all this because my grandpa Lulu who never went beyond the fifty square metres of his allotment could describe nature as knowledgeably as the globe-trotting von Humboldt. So I listen to and consult the sources around me, just as I talked to the waves as a child, and yes, it's true, Ubac has added to this discussion group. It's not about sanctity but availability, and some will call this an epiphany, perhaps a sacrilege, but I prefer this brand of sacrilege to crushing indifference and the illusion of omniscience.

Without lecturing me, Ubac lets me know that experiencing nature starts with describing it as it is, badmouthing it. I either turn it into some distant, fantasised object of fear – and we know how people are tempted to respond when they're afraid: they don't get anywhere. Or I refer to it only as part of my navel-gazing: a backdrop for selfies, an activity park, food for the soul, in other words a resource at my service, something I've appropriated. It's high time I put it back where it belongs.

And this learning process is another reason I cherish these walks and the nature around us, be it discreet or immersive. Ubac leads me from one archipelago to another, taking me by the hand, showing me how to be absorbed and teaching me this invaluable courtesy: being polite to mother nature. Aha, now I see the German roots in this Latin type – he's quite the romantic Friedrich teaching me about the great connections between the elements. If walking to heel on the lead through the packed streets of Lyon reassures him – and who can tell? – well, lying next to him on the stony ground at Parozan is an initiation for me. Our mentoring of each other balances out and this to and fro sits well with the way I see our relationship. So life is really quite simple: we just need to be together, outside and attentive. I can't think of a better barometer.

Ubac settled for the night between our two sleeping bags.

He growled loudly during the course of the starry night. We told him everything was fine and went back to sleep.

The following morning, the caretaker at the Presset refuge showed us something just a hundred and fifty metres from our bivouac: a straight line of oval depressions in the snow. The notorious wolf.

If having Ubac by our sides gives us this gift, reawakening us to fairy tales, then let's keep walking through enchanted forests for all time. I'm sure Ubac will introduce us to the elves one day.

# 17

# A growing family

There are things in life that are like Swingball. You can wallop them fervently to drive them away so they never come back but you know deep down the more effort you put into it, the less likely you are to get rid of the thing.

The way people project on to their dogs doesn't escape this rule. Mathilde and I do our best to treat Ubac like a dog, it's the least we can do, but the pretension of anthropomorphism is hard to shake off and comes back with a vengeance. Living alongside him establishes a creeping conviction that our minds are aligned to the point of being alike, and the idea of them being joined isn't unappealing – surely, getting closer to one another is what relationships are all about? Beyond their schooldays, no one goes around being an eagle, carving through the air with their arms spread wide, or thinks of themselves as a wolf; if that poetry persists it's seen as madness. I admit that I'm happy to be tempted by mimicry: I imagine Ubac's inner world and lump it together with my own, I use canine reasoning and make him think like a human. The procedure's contagious, Mathilde does it too.

And why not? Who decreed in their moth-eaten wisdom that animals were so far removed from humans, lacking in this and that, in emotions, in elation or some other emotional monopoly of ours, making any comparison meaningless? Well, it was a human, of course. Raising the bar, calling us the best – that's a game with heavily weighted dice.

Docteur Bibal and his fellow vets claim, among other things, that dogs have no sense of time and are therefore spared its emotional satellites: loneliness, boredom and insecurity. An hour is the same as a minute. Well, they should come to the chalet one morning when we're going out and leaving Ubac; they can see him downcast, his spirit buried in the depths of the earth. He's probably playing it up, but no creature could fake distress so accurately without having explored its structure. The vets should come one evening when we're reunited and watch him jump off the ground and turn circles as if coming back to life, and then curl up and sleep like a log with the comfort of being together again.

And if, as they claim, he has no notion of time, Ubac does have some idea of space. He has precisely mapped Le Châtelet. If he can't find us in the house, he'll head up to the barn from the top balcony, the one lit by the sun in the east, he'll run hard enough to make the old cider barrels shudder, peep into the barn through gaps in the planks then, seeing no one, go back down, passing the *bachal* water tank and taking the lower balcony, where the roar of the wind sounds like the sea, and he'll end up at the little stone outbuilding, the *mazot*, to see if we're there doing a bit of DIY or gathering a few walnuts. Seeing no one, he'll retrace his steps, have another look through the glass door – you never know – and nip down to the cellar which is always open and is cool even in August. Convinced he's missed us, he'll repeat the circuit two or three times then, resigned, he'll station himself under the chalet's engraved ridge beam and gaze into the distance. If he still sees no one and knows he's alone, he'll activate his nose so that his sense of smell can play its part in the investigation, then he'll come back to the front door, lie down under the *cortena* porch and heave a disconsolate sigh that can be heard right down in the valley. Every time he hears an engine, he'll run to the corner of the chalet on the Mirantin side, then traipse back dejectedly. Don't try telling me he's happy like this, or even neutral. Has anyone actually been inside a dog's heart?

Twenty years later there'll be cameras all round houses, outside and inside. Anxious owners will be alerted to their pet's every move by a beep on their phones. They'll check the screen, which they love doing, and they'll know. As it always does, an image will kill the

imaginary. In the meantime, we just imagine. Sometimes that's charming, but not always. When we leave
the chalet at three in the morning to go skiing at Lex
Blanche, we leave Ubac outside for the rest of the night
and the day. Some people say you should establish a
routine when you're leaving, a word or a gesture; others
say all this does is amplify the stress of separation –
well, who knows? Saying, 'We're coming back, you look
after the house,' is our only little habit but he knows
long before this twaddle and will even go and skulk in
a corner. It works: that's when we rate ourselves among
the ten most cruel people on the planet.

During the course of the day, if the fancy takes
us, we can imagine roe deer paying him a lovely visit
or him inviting the neighbour's hunting dog over to
whisper sweet nothings to her. But it's his loneliness
we think about mostly, a day can go by slowly. Ubac
doesn't have books or worry beads to pass the time,
much less any plans . . . dreams? Let's hope so. I'm sure
he wanders, waits, gets bored, keeps watch, feels afraid
and mopes. Convincing ourselves his inner world is a
vacuum would be convenient, but we know he's made
up of a thousand pieces and loneliness reverberates
through all of them. And if we were killed in an avalanche, who would feed him this evening? It's at about
seven o'clock, two cups filled to the brim and another
bowl for fresh water.

When we get home, he's at that same corner of the

house. He rushes over, probes his nose through the first
door to open, whimpering from having been worried;
the longer we've been away, the louder and flatter he
sings – absence can be measured just like happiness.
He races from one side of the car to the other, hardly
giving us a chance to get out, jumping up at us, scratching us, wrapping himself around us and ricocheting
for joy; dogs never hold a grudge. He's never in a bad
mood with us, forcing us to decode the reason behind
it, a sick game that people love playing as soon as you
pay them less attention. We ourselves try to normal-
ise these reunions, thinking this trick will help soften
the blow of the next separation. Without much success:
the whole thing ends with us all rolling on the ground
saying we love each other, the only valid ritual we have
here. Then we sleep, intoxicated with contentment.

The idea isn't to stop going away – no love requires you
to be trapped for its sake – but then what to do? Confronted with this stomach-churning problem, arithmetic comes to the rescue: when there are two, it tells
us, they're not as lonely as just one.

Why not have more dogs? What better than the same
species with the identical language to combat loneliness? The swifts and hares and other passing life forms
aren't enough. Another dog, yes, that's the simplest
solution, but we can already tell that, in practice, it
won't feel so simple. We may need to convince ourselves

and protect our decision from looking like a whim, but Mathilde and I are experts at tipping the balance with what appears to be an overview. There's Ubac's imagined loneliness – an idea that would make other people laugh – and our guilt at perpetuating it. There are the packs of street dogs seen in Sighetu in Romania or Meteora in Greece, gorgeous wild dogs whose restlessness seems to be quashed by their sheer numbers. There's also a hint of animism that sometimes lulls us; if Ubac were to contradict his immortality and die, his soul would come to rest in the nearest thing, in the body of another dog that had shared his bed and this would keep him close to us. An imagined imprinting that would prolong him and comfort us. Why not.

We went to get the first new addition in Gleizé out of a sort of loyalty to France's low population 'diagonal'. A tiny sand-coloured Labrador a bit like Ïko. She was advertised in the 69, sold by travellers – a promising concept – not far from the vineyards of Beaujolais – also promising – raised with less cosseting than Ubac but with enough love to make her reluctant to leave her home, including her mother. You never get used to these wrenches. Her date of birth was quite dubious, the vet's stamp even more so and we paid cash as with all slightly dodgy deals. Three hundred euros, a third of what Ubac had cost.

When we return from this kidnapping which didn't

involve him, Ubac throws himself at the driver's door as usual, there's little danger of finding no one on that side, putting both his front paws on the edge of the window. He's barely started his hellos when his eyes and nose identify the pale little thing on the other seat, and Mathilde is immediately ignored. He springs over to the other side, runs round and round again, almost gets run over, scratches both doors ten times, his front paws no longer touching the ground, so he looks like Corsican goats that prefer low-hanging branches to grass. The little white thing is barely half awake when it realises it won't be alone in our human world. We only have time to lower the window before they breathe each other's smell for the first time. And first times are always a delicate balance; of course, you have to experience them to the full and soon try to detach yourself from them, separate yourself with an intense focus or some other process that will bury them deep in the memory. The very fact that there are several of us could help.

We call her Cordée – it means a roped team, a group of climbers roped together, so there's a mountain reference and it implies they'll look after each other. We've willingly given in to something we find crass in other people when they call their dogs John, Paul, Ringo and Co.; perhaps we misguidedly believe that mountain climbing will always be a less futile passion. Cordée weighs nothing, her coat's very pale except for her ears, she has a graceful little body, translucent claws, an oblong head and eyelashes like a Hollywood actress. She's as well turned out as her enclosure was grubby. When she's happy – which is almost always – she wags furiously, her whole body a comma shape, we're almost worried she'll break herself in two as her dense tail plays the tambourine. She finds this tail entertaining, grabbing it with her mouth, and together they turn circles, undertake acrobatics and take tumbles. Ubac hasn't sniffed her back end; he followed her everywhere, and now – addled by all the coming and going – he's sat down on a promontory where he can catch every part of this high-speed show. Meanwhile, Cordée comes and goes without a moment's respite, then slams on the brakes, crouches down and rears up tall in search of him: she looks like a meerkat. When she comes back and clings to him, he pretends not to be interested. Together they're already quite a performance: one dog is a photo, two make a film. Our idea for filling the empty hours is keeping its promises.

That same evening, Mathilde and I go out to drink to this new arrival, accompanied by our big dog and his little acolyte who we want to introduce to everyone. We choose the first bar we come to, it's like any other bar with a counter, tables, forgotten music, and a few people further down the road to drunkenness than others. We choose to sit outside, the best option for people with dogs. We've only just sat down when an intrepid mutt appears out of nowhere wanting to get to know Cordée. He comes closer, right up to her innocent backside and Ubac, stationed like a bodyguard slightly to one side but very nearby, pings awake from his fake sleep, jumps up and catapults the other dog with no warning. Any other animals now know the price to pay if they dare approach this ivory-coloured treasure.

A few days later, Cordée is sleeping peacefully on the chalet's terrace and Ubac is on the move, which is unusual. In the last few minutes, he alone has noticed the manoeuvres of a kite circling the house. From where it's soaring, little Cordée looks like very white and very serene prey. Ubac growls, then barks a clear, meaningful bark. We go outside and when the raptor makes its nosedive, it finds itself confronted with a tri-colour security guard and two naive humans. That little puppy came very close to flying away for ever. How lovely it must be to be introduced to the world under Ubac's protectorate.

Ubac teaches Cordée some of the basics of everyday life, as Tchoumi did him – life is just an endless rosary of legacies. She remembers some, such as the exact time they're fed minus fifteen minutes, and how to make efficient use of big brown eyes. In exchange, she teaches him how to swim fearlessly in mountain streams: she plays around, he gets worried, jumps in, hops from stone to stone and roars at her to stop, she only listens for a minute. She can do anything to him – chew his neck, dump a rotten apple on his nose, rootle around in his bowl, go to sleep on his flank – he doesn't make a fuss. On the rare occasions when she oversteps the mark, he curls back his lips and puts together a growling sound, she cowers contritely; fear and aggression are both performed to perfection. She's been accepted: Ubac prefers sharing to jealousy and in return he gets extra helpings of affection – it's a lesson worth remembering. Looking across the meadows we can see a black dog and a white periscope wagging happily; fate had the choice of thousands of other dogs but it's her and him, and nothing else is imaginable.

It may be only in our eyes that Ubac's status has changed, but he's really like a father. This puppy who still isn't putting on weight – we could play the xylophone on her ribs and have to remind doubters that she eats her fill – isn't a second Ubac but a separate entity that apes him and complements him and stands apart from him. She is his long-time daughter who will become his sister but never his courtesan – sometimes dogs do consider what would or wouldn't be appropriate. When it comes to being truly alike, the pair have an infallible trick: they find a stagnant pond and clothe themselves in offensive sludge, both the same brown and dripping with satisfaction, amazed to be shooed away at the doorstep and turning to look at each other as if indicating which of them came up with this brilliant idea. Life at home has become twice as turbulent, the placid Ubac is reinvigorated by this effervescent pup who's determined to snap up every lizard, every minute life offers, and seems to be equipped with an inexhaustible resistance to boredom. It's wonderful to watch them living their lives, bundles of black and white fur blending in an exuberant circus that never turns to grey.

All this could suppress our anthropomorphism, but it still comes back in waves to pick a fight. Even if this does mean attributing human emotions to animals, we go so far as assuming Ubac feels something that's inconceivable to the two of us: an appetite for true parenthood. How modern of us! Ubac with an adoptive daughter from a very different background, plus a biological baby; a single-parent family taken on by the father, with these tattooed not-too-ancient grandparents who live half the time in a van. We're taken with the idea, the main shortcoming in our relationship being that there's no moderator to temper the other's enthusiasms. As for Ubac and Cordée, neither of them protests.

Ubac has already done the deed with a bitch in the village. When Michel, a friend from Arêches, invited us to help take his cows up to their summer pasture, we took Ubac with us. He wasn't very interested in the cattle – oh, if his herding ancestors had seen him! On the other hand, he was fantastically successful at distracting Titoune, a border collie, from her cowgirl tasks for a brief but deeply felt tryst which, we learned a few months later, had resulted in a litter of handsome mongrels. The puppies had been distributed here and there among local farmers, which meant that we viewed all tricolour dogs on the mountains with grandparental tenderness. Michel often complained that the Beaufortain area was being depopulated; well, Ubac had zealously applied himself to countering this exodus.

We now need to find a bitch who's willing, a Bernese Mountain Dog – just this once we're subscribing to the appeal of keeping it in the breed family. It's not easy: with no coffee machines, salsa clubs or mutual friends, dogs don't have many matchmaking institutions. At best, a series of walks synchronise over several days; a yellow Kangoo always parks in the same place by the pond at about six in the evening and a bitch hops out. We pass on our walks several times, eventually say hello, get to know her name, there's some sniffing between the dogs, some fraternising, but not enough to imagine starting a family. So we need to be pragmatic about this and make a meeting happen soon by advertising. After all, humans can bring about love too.

'Urgent. Very beautiful 7-year-old Bernese Mountain Dog seeks girl for mating.' Although we toyed for ages with *reproduction* as the punchline, this was the best wording we could come up with. The good thing about these few words, accompanied by a photo of Ubac standing heroically on a mountaintop, is that they're explicit and they suggest that the relationship won't go beyond a bit of productive congress. We stick up posters pretty much everywhere we go, alongside ones of lost dogs, with our phone number written in large print, like ads on traffic lights in city centres.

We don't have to wait long; we'd underestimated the market. The first date takes place at the chalet, the in-laws were keen to make the journey. A man with a shiny pate and a clamped jaw travelled a long way with his dog to meet Ubac. We hadn't anticipated this, but it's quite chilling. There's a lurking sense of the prescriptive archaic practice of arranged marriages, of forceful human intervention and, let's say it as it is, a nasty taste of prostitution. Mathilde and I are uncomfortable, and the only thing that convinces us to keep going is that both dogs are enthusiastic. Their nuptial dance is quite simple with the young lady in front and Ubac behind, like her shadow. Then on top. Cordée, who's too young for this show, is outside sniffing chanterelles. The apogee of good taste is that we have to watch them, oversee them – apparently the end of the procedure can be dramatic – as if they need us, as if we're experts in handling the reproductive process. Everything goes as it should and the man leaves with his dog. The mood's light-hearted, I tell Ubac it was our turn anyway – he's watched us often enough, the lecher. Six weeks later, the man sends us a blunt message, saying: 'It didn't

work, my bitch isn't in pup.' Mathilde and I are convinced he's lying and is making money out of his dog's
charms. We should have studied body language which
never lies: the man didn't look his dog in the eye or put
his arms around her. We give up on the tawdry idea of
orchestrating a coupling.

Luckily, fate – as usual – arranges things nicely
and is a more appropriate agent than coldly calculated
dates. One day when we're walking near the pond at
Marcôt, Ubac, who has a broken toe at the time and
isn't allowed to run, spots an elegant Bernese Mountain
Dog in the distance and hurries over to her, despite
our disapproving cries – this must be what his lead's
for. We strike up conversation, he's recognised as the
dog in the ad, just as handsome in real life. Alpine (yes,
that's her name – you don't get many dogs named after
the sea in these parts) and Ubac see each other several
times and this is less and less by chance, they meet at
his house or hers, like a pair of besotted high-schoolers
with supportive parents. We find them stuck together
back-to-back twice and cry alleluia, and five weeks after
these intriguing 'ties', Docteur Wicky tells us there are
four puppies on the way. We hesitate to flaunt the scan
photo in front of our friends who still can't understand
why we don't want children, but in private it sends us
into paroxysms of excitement.

Nature doesn't always work perfectly, though,
because two of the puppies die at birth, and these

early stages are all about survival: for Alpine who pulls through fine but whose agonised expression still haunts us, and for the two remaining puppies who made it by the skin of their teeth and whose first few days will only just be helped by the plethora of available teats. The letter for the year is F. Alpine's family keep a dog puppy, Falco, more in honour of a local mayor Hubert Falco than the Roman Catholic monsignor of the same name. The bitch puppy, Frison, joins us when she's two months old. She's recovered from too much, far too much not to resent us for so desperately wanting this life. On the exact same day Tchoumi dies . . . whether it's a vacuum or doubling, nature abhors something. In the early weeks, all we see is a mini-Ubac, but soon, luckily, Frison reminds us that every creature deserves better than to be seen only in comparison to another, and that having a model doesn't preclude departures in unanticipated directions. She's inherited his discreet blaze but everything else about her is less restrained, which is a good thing. As for Cordée, she adores this ever-ready new toy.

Frison's best way to distinguish herself from her father is to disobey everything, so we constantly, uninhibitedly yell her name, which can produce angry reactions in the villages of the Beaufortain, homeland of the illustrious mountaineer Roger Frison-Roche; but you never know, there may still be some little streets where the explorer's name hasn't been heard.

# 18

# A perfect number

Life as a clan of five takes shape and is joyously unconstrained.

It takes pretty flawless precision to get three good-sized dogs into a van, remember the right food for one, the medication for another or to plan the logistics of who'll look after them in our absence – exactly the sort of thing you're avoiding when you choose to live as free as the wind. It's still an engaging bedlam, with dogs everywhere, in every room, simultaneous or successive comings and goings, mass excitement over some small initiative shown by one of them, an exquisite mazurka making the whole household nod along from first light, punctuated with no warning by collective naps when nothing moves, except for the odd creaking floorboard.

There's a music to it too, a music all their own that no sound engineer could ever capture. The percussion of their tours of inspection around the rickety balcony. Their snoring to the power of three in the van on a night in the wild. The way they bound in and out of the van – all that's missing are the hoops of fire. The clank as their bowls knock together. The sound of them lapping their water – together because Cordée drinks only when Ubac does. The tips of their tails beating a rhythm on the floor, their dream cycles relayed from one to the other. Their choreographed reaction to the slightest sound in the distance: Cordée gives the first warning, sniffing the air and waiting for backup, Frison comes running with ear-splitting yaps, Ubac brings up the rear with his swagger and his cavernous voice, approaching the next supposed assailant – which could be a delivery driver or maybe the sound barrier!

Then there are their play fights. Their chain-reaction disobedience. The medley of their bodies waiting for us on the ground, and as soon as we lie down, slumping on to us in a heap. The tangle of their leads when we're in busy cities. Our affectionate pandemonium. And all the things we'll remember when they're gone. I think that's what we want: background noise and days filled with even more of the tumult of interconnected lives.

The appeal of pack life invites questions. With four dogs, or ten, would the group happiness lose its lustre? Does this appetite have limits as others do, and are excesses sickening? There are limits, yes, they're emerging and measurable and go by the names of financial reality, finite living space and the certainty that, whatever shepherds may say of their sheep, an individual gets swamped and loses themselves in a group over a certain size.

Having three dogs first and foremost reminds us we each have only one pair of hands, that standard gauge of available love. You could add to that our heads, toes and whole bodies; it's quite a performance satisfying their every look, every proffered paw because the three of them inevitably want affection at the same time or if one of them has the idea first, the other two immediately show up. If we ever stroke only one of our dogs, it will mean the other two have passed on.

More than three would be a waste. It's easy to picture happiness being contagious, but with skipping stones the final bounces are rather limp, and I feel there's the same attrition with love: up to a particular threshold, it shares itself out and then, confronted with so many hearts to sustain, it loses its way, runs out of energy or, worse, chooses. So three and two seems like the right arithmetic, availability all round, the happiness of the group as a whole and nothing too symmetrical. Not to mention, André tells me, that five isn't the worst of numbers, it's how many senses we have, how many fingers we have and the number of Enid Blyton's *Famous Five*, in which Timmy plays more than a supporting role and does his damnedest to be like the humans. So, Mathilde, let's stop trying to be clever with happiness, there are times when it digs in its heels. And don't let's forget that Ubac takes looking after the other two very seriously and we don't want to burden him with any more responsibilities.

We spend a lot of time watching them live their lives – a TV salesman wouldn't make his fortune at Le Châtelet. There's something to watch every minute, something soothing, stimulating or supportive, depending on what's needed. They're never apart, except when one of them goes to the vet, and then the patient's homecoming is celebrated by the other two as if they've miraculously survived the Great War.

Often – too often for me with my penchant for unity – I have to get up early to go to work far away, too far away. A minor bother but it does bother me. It's about five in the morning and I'm creeping out of the bedroom so as not to wake Mathilde. 'Put the light on if you want,' she says, but I get dressed in the hall. As I step into the main room, there's a creaky floorboard which alerts the gang. Mending it is on next century's to-do list. That's what you get with doing up an old house: you move heaven and earth for months on end, you're on first-name terms with the forklift operators at the local builders' suppliers, then one day, with no warning, it's over and even changing a light bulb is too much. Then you have to wait – and you'll be counting in months or perhaps for ever – for your motivation to be restocked. The three dogs have the whole room but sleep mostly welded together, a box room would more than do for them. Cordée looks at me through one half-open eye, beats out her two-time rhythm; Frison and Ubac pretend they haven't heard anything, but the hang of their feather-duster tails gives them away; their tails are like their hearts – they can't be controlled.

I open the hatch in the fireplace a fraction and the fire comes back to life. I put on another log, whose embers Mathilde will see later, the water boils, my tea's brewing and yesterday's bread is toasting, it all smells great. The revived licks of flame light the room with a kaleidoscope of dancing shadows; I mustn't break the spell, and definitely won't put the light on. I could get up later, but this moment makes all the short nights worth it. I watch the dogs half-sleeping, there's not one morning when I'm not moved by their gentle harmony – could any one of them actually live alone? In the night the bed mats have been swapped, shared, rolled around and moved about, but everything seems calm. I go over to them each in turn and say hello with a hand on a flank, a kiss in the crook of a neck, and receive just a paw in exchange. They all know I'm coming or going, and every morning I change which one I touch first to change which one comes last. I inhale their smell to my deepest alveoli, stealing it inside me.

When I cut the bread, Frison – the greedy one – stretches. Tickled by the first delicious aromas, her nose quivers and she comes over to ask how my night was. This dog has an avowed passion for eating and deems everything edible, from oven gloves to wallets, so it's good news that she's showing an interest in a recognised foodstuff. She licks the air frenetically, thinking this will suck in a few particles of bread, and puts her head on my thigh, confident she can get anything out of me if she tilts her eyes up at me. I tell her to make the most of it because firm rules are starting next week. Cordée comes next, thanks her sister the scout for opening the way and puts her head on the same thigh. Bits of crust migrate and are hardly chewed – André would love this – my trousers are decorated with specks of drool, I should consider wearing overalls for breakfast. Ubac and his patriarchal delay come to join us and, in a minutely detailed ballet, he rests his huge head on the other two, making full use of his eyes from the angle at which he's parked himself. Then I put my arms around all three of them as if going into a scrum. For anyone who thinks they have the monopoly on happiness, this is probably just a cute scene. But for me, as I get covered in their guard hairs, it gives me a whole day's worth of contentment and mettle to cope with the world and keep it at bay.

Then, if time allows, we go for a walk. We disturb a few nocturnal creatures. Thanks to my headlamp, I spot the slightly anxious eyes of a roe buck retreating to his sleeping quarters in the distance. Animals may be right to be wary of all humans, but I so wish they knew that some of us will never hurt them. Not one of the dogs chases after it – there's a pact. We hear a snapping sound deep in the woods; if it's a man, I would know. These mornings are quite a sight, the last stars, the first glimmers of light, the silences devoid of fear – it all adds to their beauty. The prevailing mood is of wholeness and a sense of eternity, something like transcendence but with no Father or substance. Sometimes snow has fallen in the chill of the night, virgin of footsteps except for a few hare prints. The threesome want to play; I tell them I don't have time without really understanding why I don't devote my whole life to playing. We go back to the house, and they return to one or other bed mat, apparently chosen at random.

It's at this point that I look questioningly at Ubac; he'll tell me unambiguously whether he'd like to come with me or stay with the ladies. I always hope he'll get up to follow me but know how anxious the trio are whenever one element is missing. He can do what he likes, he's essentially free, and he comes about half the time, but in terms of who misses who, the balance isn't entirely symmetrical. When I leave on my own, I can cry – with happiness, anger or a bit of everything. I point the van up the track from the chalet, it's as steep as a take-off. And yes, I'm tearing myself away from my grounding.

We've relinquished our original idea of populating the world with Ubacs – which was so well intentioned but hypocritical – and anyway, we'd got something wrong:

when we leave all three of them behind, plans to lighten the burden of guilt for abandoning a single dog are a total failure. Six eyes make it clear that a threesome will always be less than all five of us, all that counts is the whole group and we now have to come to terms with this collective loneliness. They take turns to play the role of the condemned individual, and the other two play the tearful family. It works quite well: leaving without drowning in remorse takes all Mathilde's or my resolve, and when neither of us can summon it, we put our bags back down and that's that.

If their group mentality unwittingly plays on our weaknesses, it also has its strengths: it protects, nurtures and fortifies the individuals. It's a pleasing anomaly of their union that their identities aren't forgotten but enhanced. Cordée is Cordée, Frison is Frison, never reduced to companion females for a lone male dog. The relationships shift. The way we view and interpret these ties is quite unsettling: over the years Cordée seems to have taken on the role of Ubac's sister, but Frison will be his daughter till the very end – probably the power of blood ties, or the habit of attributing this role to her. By this logic, Cordée should be an aunt to Frison but they're like sisters. Basically, nothing's really fixed except the essential value they each have.

Ubac is still there, in no way diluted by the group but elevated to the rank of original being from which all things flowed, the source. *Fonte*, the Italians say, or something like that. If his and my two-sided relationship is less apparent, their unity outweighs any nostalgia; to steal an idea from Jacques Prévert, we 'interlive' with one another. Each of our dogs has its own character and its own share of copying the others' characters, there's just enough cross-pollination and it spreads to us too. Mathilde and I sometimes sniff each other's necks to get close, quietly animalising ourselves. Long-standing friends tell us these canine behaviours have been around for a while; that sort of love isn't the done thing between brothers and sisters, they joke.

We've become aware of another misconception of ours: it's absurd to think that, when one of our dogs dies, our pain will be diminished by the living memory of the other two. The heart doesn't work like that, it's no ordinary muscle, the torn fibres don't form again. Because we can now see that added to the pain of loss will be their pain and ours at no longer seeing them all together.

When Frison dies, Cordée won't be able to walk for a whole week. No vet will find a solution: scans can't detect love. She'll wobble helplessly and collapse every ten metres, her body limp and, I think, wishing it was all over. Living alone spares you a lot of pain.

Our life and the equilibrium we establish will be like this for several years. We will always have this, the strength of our gang, its excesses and disorderliness, and no turnaround can ever take away the experience of living like that. Because yes, a disorderly life is all the fuller. Surely everyone's noticed that when you stack your shopping neatly in the trolley as it's checked out, there now isn't room for all the stuff that was piled in at random before?

Through various changes, house moves, seasons and aspects of life, everything will be multiplied by three and more, and this exponential effect will set the pace for our lives. This is also true of concerns: Cordée with a limp, Frison on chemo and Ubac growing old. With three of them, there may be little let-up in happiness, but the same can be said of worries.

As with any form of self-reliance, the pleasure of being together envelops and isolates us. We only half-live everyday life, we're somewhere cut off from the world – not that we hate other people but we've retreated from them out of excess availability to the dogs. We're wary of this canine invasion and of forming an impenetrable bubble but these are encroaching realities: we're slightly withdrawing from the world. People who don't like the lively reception committees don't come to the house so much; we turn down some invitations for want of a dogsitter or for fear of being an invasion; and we postpone plans in favour of complete freedom. All contact becomes less frequent and – despite our fierce determination not to cultivate the image of loners avoiding their own kind, despite our love of people – plenty of them don't measure up in our view. Anyone who spends time on equal terms with dogs and animals in general knows they set the bar very high. This apparent disdain might seem forced, intended, but it's just a natural trajectory. 'That's how it is,' Grandpa Lulu used to say with no note of resignation. We're not suffering its effects yet; the shortcomings of isolation, if we experience any, will come later. We make some dog friends, meeting up with ten other people for collective outings in the forest, but we don't adhere much to groups, particularly if they're based on shared convictions. We always hesitate to park our van reassuringly among other camping-cars, not keen to discuss GPS, 2.3 litres and autumn in Andalucia. On close examination, we prefer life.

The same even goes for people we really like for their love of animals – the coochy-cooing and the comparative studies of omega-3 levels in dog meal are a bit wearying. In these gatherings the time always comes when one of the men – the one with the most Germanic dog – wants a photo of all ten of us, motionless, smiling and (such a nice idea) in age order. He'll never succeed. Luckily unruliness is contagious and, if need be, we'll discreetly encourage one of our three to wander out of shot. Then we regroup and set off again.

This looks fiendishly like evasion or contempt, but is it that shameful? The small community around us has done the same to us: We're '*that* couple – you know, the couple with three dogs' and this definition is fine by us because it doesn't appear to subtract anything from our lives or replace any part of them. In fact, it covers its surface with protuberances that snag everything that goes past . . . including that indefinable thing called happiness. We're so happy it frightens me. I'm sure it would be possible to die of having had too much joy, just to leave a few crumbs for everyone else. I would even think that fair.

Something about the five of us has taken root for the long term, even if only that I'll always have this slightly isolated relationship with the world. It can rejoice or crumble around us but, selfishly, we have only one safety measure: keeping the closest possible watch on our perfect sanctuary and doing a head count. Five. A perfect number whose only weakness is that it can't go on for ever, and one day, indisputably, it will go down and pick us apart. But we're battling to maintain it.

On hot summer evenings, Mathilde and I put two mattresses on the terrace at Le Châtelet and we sleep in the open surrounded by the three dogs and a few pygmy owls prepared to share the night with us. Shooting stars do their shooting and, among our guiltiest longings, we can't think of a better wish than for life to go on like this.

# PART THREE

# 19

# Road rage

It's one of those days when Ubac and I do our own thing together. A Thursday.

The ladies at Le Châtelet, the gentlemen in Belley. This gender distinction isn't our style, but we've succumbed to it today. In the mornings, Ubac has two ways of letting me know he'd like to come with me. When Cordée and Frison head down to the chalet on our way back from their short 'comfort break' walk, he lets them get ahead, pretends to saunter, then comes to a stop next to the van. If we haven't yet been out that morning, then when I come to say goodbye to each of them on their bed mats, he stands up, looks me right in the eye and tenses every muscle. I ask for confirmation, 'Do you want to come?' and he nudges the door open with his nose without so much as a 'see ya" to the household. They must have said their goodbyes earlier. I don't know what makes him decide to come, certainly not my need to have him there because that never changes.

I tell Cordée and Frison, who are now determined to follow, that I love them too, then I go through to Mathilde who's half-asleep. I don't tell *her* I love her as often as I should, assuming that demonstrating the fact is enough. Instead, I say, 'Ubac's coming with me. I'll see you this evening or tomorrow. I'll call to let you know.'

I open the side door and the passenger door of the van for Ubac and he chooses. It's the front today. I give him a bit of a push from behind but his enthusiasm does most of the work, and I'm happy to be alone with him. There's always a bag of kibble in the van. Just in case.

For the first few kilometres we listen to the morning breakfast show on France Inter, finding out what the world's up to after a night without news, and letting Thomas Legrand make us feel switched on for four minutes. We make a detour via Bourget-du-Lac, necessitated by Boulangerie Claret's chocolate chip cookies: when so many places have just external chocolate chips for show, they embed a hundred of them inside. I tell myself it would be more sensible to buy two than three . . . and take three small ones. To ease my conscience and my stomach, I give half of one to my copilot, and to hell with the ban on dark chocolate, Ubac's securely enough anchored to life to have no worries about a few grams of theobromine. There's now an empty bag and a lot of crumbs in the front of the van and Marvin Gaye's got my hips swaying – a pleasing mess. In a few minutes I'll be walking through the staff-room but for now I'm full of a joy that's oblivious to life's problems.

I park near the sports halls. While the students are going through to the changing rooms, I open the door for Ubac who knows he needs to be discreet and lies down next to the van. From there under the weeping willows, he watches my middle-distance running class across the sports field. Students exempted from the class, who've usually been assigned blatantly boring chores, are allowed to hang out with him – weirdly, the number of sprains and asthmatic tendencies goes up week on week.

At break time, when the young are released to their canoodling and their fights, Ubac and I go for a rather quick walk on our own. I'd like Ubac to defecate at 10.30 precisely like a good civil servant, but his gut exercises its right to insubordination. Colleagues watch me through the window. 'You prefer dogs to people, don't you?' the French teacher will ask me for the fifteenth time and, for the fifteenth time, I play along with her game and quote from Molière's *Mis-anthrope* with a *We value nothing if we value everyone.* Then it's javelin with the Year 10s, a lesson that earns me a flatteringly high mark from Ubac for my teaching skills: the children seem to be happy playing, which is his only criterion in deciding what's worth teaching.

At lunchtime, we drop in to say hello to Jacqueline and André. I miss them, my adoptive grandparents, the only sort I have left. I still sometimes sleep in the annexe when the prospect of the trip back to Beaufort is too exhausting. I wish they too could go on for ever, we'd have no trouble filling infinity. This Thursday, my plate's waiting for me, a lovingly prepared meal as usual, meat in a delicious buttery or creamy sauce. I still haven't dared tell them I'm vegetarian – they're so familiar with hardship they wouldn't understand. A carnivorous accomplice under my chair helps me avoid offending them. Blueberry tart, coffee and a nip of *vulnéraire* that never killed anyone, then the Carrels and Ubac join forces to ask whether he can stay with them for the afternoon. Of course.

I pick him back up at about six o'clock. I've still got the time and the energy to go home to the girls so I politely decline André's offer of a small Pernod which, as I recall, is never that small, is noticeably short on water and would keep me here.

Ubac jumps into the front again and we set off, heading home. A radio show called *One Day in the World* reminds us how varied and fragile our world is. When we reach the Virignin roundabout, the first of the journey, a sort of pick-up truck arrives to our right at the same time as us; I can see it's slowing so I drive on. They had the same idea, we both brake sharply, making the tyres squeal. As a fatherly reflex, I put my arm out in front of my passenger, as if one hand could stop forty-five kilos. The occupants of the other vehicle, two young guys, toot furiously, gesticulate at me – including one extremely upstanding middle finger – and shout, like so many people emboldened by being in a vehicle. I lower the window to tell them I love them too (not a response that will save the world, and this evening, sheepish for stooping so low, I'll promise to come to terms with my mistakes). It usually ends like this, macho men beating their chests to prove to themselves that they're the strongest, then going home and each relating an inflated story that makes them out as the hero.

I drive on and they follow close behind me, stick to my bumper, pull out, pull back in and flash their lights at me. They must have seen that I'm on my own. Our stupidity and courage crank up a notch. We drive between the cliffs of the Gorges de la Balme then to Yenne where the sky reappears, and they're still at it – group mentality is rarely a good thing.

Eventually I've had enough. I mean, are they planning to follow me all the way home? Being a well-brought-up driver, I put on my indicator and pull into a little lay-by. A rustic sign recommends taking a break and insists no litter be dropped. The two cowboys follow me but braking hard as if in a Clint Eastwood film. 'Those two really are morons,' I tell Ubac. Well, you have to use the words to hand and with some people it's not worth trying to find better.

For once, the anger is stepping out of the vehicles: I get out, they get out and we end up between the two trucks. One of them's wearing a *faluche*, a type of beret favoured by socially insecure medical students who make idiots of themselves on Malibu. The logic of testosterone steps on to the stage, reminding me of makeshift parties from years ago when – after the Clash, some pogoing and a few white-wine-and-lemonades at three francs a pop – we'd fight that evening's enemy: rugby players versus the inner-city lads, one high school against another, the different hopefuls for a girl called Séverine . . . boozy nights when we gave the best of ourselves to some crappy cause.

These guys have blood-red eyes, implying a far from normal state – not a good sign. It's not the real them I'm dealing with, and their alter-egos may be fearless. We start talking, then yelling at each other, each trying to establish that he's right, he's the strongest and his opponent needs to back down – an alpha male thing. The guy who I'm guessing is the leader and I get so close our foreheads are touching, like footballers but not so equally matched; the second guy, I can tell, is gradually sidling behind me. When I was a child, anyone who attacked from behind was banished from future scuffles and they could dream on if they thought they'd ever get chips in the canteen again. All minor news stories must start like this, with nothing much, with little blokes posturing, then comes the rush, then comes pride until there's no stopping them. Who needs hardened criminals or real hatred – ordinary men can manage this fine on their own.

The first guy grabs my collar, I do the same and we shove each other backwards for the first time. 'Chill out!' he yells, looking anything but chilled himself. His sidekick sort of clips me on the back of the neck as you would an unruly child, while the first guy and I grab each other again, harder, more determined. Backtracking's no longer really an option, it's going to end badly with one or other of us on the ground, defeated, begging for it to be over and apologising. Dozens of cars drive past.

It's when we strike the first two blows that he appears.

Ubac's there. I have time to think it's impossible because he was in the front and both doors were shut. This contributes to the surreal feeling. He barks, making a sound I've never heard from him before, and telling the two men to stop if they value their lives. He lunges at the first guy, the obvious leader, his priority, and shoves into him with a sound like a heavy door, then coolly shows him all his teeth. The guy's on the ground, a good three metres away, his head thwacked down hard. If he comes back for more, he'll lose a lump of flesh, from a thigh or his throat. Ubac takes two steps forward, his tail horizontal, his teeth bared, part dog and part wolf. Gobsmacked and afraid of being killed, both men have frozen.

'Call off your dog, call him off, I said!'

'Or what?'

It's easy to think these battles are ridiculous, but when you gain the upper hand, you start to see the attractions.

Ubac looks from one to the other, his hackles up, his front feet hardly touching the ground, his haunches ready to leap and his lips retracted as far as they'll go. He's showing that he could kill and that, in the canine justice system, it's a conceivable sentence. He's keeping them at bay, keeping them in their place. He's stopped barking now but growls powerfully, from deep in his belly, it's even more terrifying. The intimidation phase is over, the only available option now is action.

It occurs to me that I'm not in control of my dog, and it's true: this dog isn't really mine. The sidekick stammers that he's scared and very slowly creeps into their truck. I hope he pissed himself. I'm worried he'll come back out with a weapon, a metal bar or God knows what to hurt Ubac. A car slows down and watches us – will they get the wrong idea of who's attacking who? The leader also retreats to the truck, backing slowly and swearing about how lucky I am and how he'll find me, and I won't always have my piece-of-shit mutt with me. I want to smash his face in for insulting Ubac. They leave the same way they came, violently, flicking fingers through the window and in a noisy cloud of dust.

Everything falls silent, Ubac calms down, his limbs relax instantly. He finally knows what to do with violence – he'll do without. He immediately turns to something else, sniffs around, pees here, pees there, then wants to go for a walk. My first thought is to get away. He's not trumpeting any sort of victory, not puffing any part of his anatomy, not overplaying anything; if I'd been the victor I'd have done two laps of honour by now. The fact is that he's an animal. I need to walk, get my heart rate back down and get rid of this crushing feeling on my ribcage.

I go to park the van straighter and discover how Ubac got out: one window was slightly open, halfway at best, let's say forty centimetres. A jump from the front seat down on to the tarmacked ground, I don't under-stand how it's physically possible. That night I'll dream he's walking through walls. After a jump like that, I need to inspect his knees, like checking over a soldier after an attack. He lets me look at them, generously allowing me to think he needs me. We set off along a little path. Amazing how good silence is for you, how soothing nature is. I prefer its brand of violence to ours; here everything feels new and promising. I think of his nerve, his courage, all the excuses there were for him to be afraid. Ubac's a little way away ahead now; I call him and he comes back. How does this knight contemplate obeying me? The world's built back to front.

I knew it, I proclaimed it to all who would listen, even the deaf, and it really is true.

Ubac is prepared to die for me.

## 20

# Gone

On Thursday 13 July 2017, at about one in the afternoon, I think, Ubac died.

A few seconds earlier, he was alive.

I've been told he was lying on his left side. After
millions of cycles, the right flank rose very high, his
ribs – which had become so prominent – flared; the
last centilitres of air, good air, passed through; his ribs
subsided and then nothing more. There are things like
breathing that we do by the truckload without realising
that one day we'll do them for the very last time. Do we
end on an inhalation or an exhalation? It must depend
on what we want: to keep going or to leave. There must
have been a sigh, the crickets will have fallen silent in
homage and then resumed their chirping, and maybe,
just before this, Ubac looked at the world around him
and captured it for all time. The meadow opposite,
empty of cows now gone to their summer grazing, and
scorched under a lead-blue sky – that's the last view

life offered him, this dog who so loved winter. His soul vanished in an instant, a puffball exploding and its golden dust settling as close as possible to the living. Cordée and Frison felt a breath spread through them like a draught of black honey. Meanwhile, I was eating dessert and I think we were laughing.

A few minutes earlier, Ubac did a visual check round. He made sure there were no anxious humans nearby – a life devoted to graciousness remains that way even down to its departure. He turned his head from left to right and his eyes scanned from one end of his field of vision the other, he sniffed his immediate surroundings, it was all his body could still do. My parents had been nipping up regularly from the floor below to check he was still among the living, they moved his limbs, picked off the gravel stuck to his jowls and moistened them, patted his bones, told him he was a good dog and prayed for it to be over. My parents are readily available both for easy celebrations and difficult tasks, and this versatility is a measure of absolute love. My mother must already have been sad because I was sad, to the point of forgetting her own right to be. She was already wondering whether, in the event, she should let us know and how. Jean-Pierre said it would be better to wait till we got back otherwise we'd end up in the ditch and that would be game, set and match.

They'd just been up to see him, Ubac had a free hand

and half an hour in which to die. That's how he wanted his exit to be. Peacefully alone. He summoned Cordée and Frison, happy for his two girls who understand the hereafter to be part of the moment, and whispered a few words for them to say to us every day in the future. They licked his muddy nose, to make him present-able, and soon knew they were alone, and that it was for ever; they whined. Their company was enough and just what he wanted.

I keep bombarding my mind with this conviction to give myself the strength to keep going. There are fleeting, violent, invasive thoughts where I picture him horribly alone, writhing in this abandoned state, grap-pling with his fear and our cowardly indifference, and I do my best to dismiss these invitations to join him. I was seventy-eight kilometres away; it could have been one or ten thousand – I wasn't there. I'd put my phone on the edge of the table while we ate and kept checking it compulsively. My hosts teased me for this teenage-like obsession; I hadn't told them anything, it wasn't their problem. I'd given my parents a special ringtone, my ears were on high alert and every part of me palpi-tated at each notification. After a few minutes in the blazing sun, the screen announced it was overheating and I immediately put my wretched iPhone back in the shade. That pause lasted twenty minutes. Meanwhile, Mathilde had broken down on the side of the road, the turbo had given up. That dog's powers extended to making use of our machines to keep us away long enough for the grim tableau.

A few hours earlier I'd wondered, what's the point of going for this lunch? What event in my spectacular, mediocre life would justify leaving my dog? Not one. Then Ubac started eating, gulping down some overcooked pasta, when he hadn't wanted anything for two days. He'd had something to drink, just a little from my mouth. His expression had emerged from the depths, and he'd batted me gently with one paw. In his downward curve of deterioration, this was a sort of hillock, the P wave on an ECG. It was his last effort: convincing me this would go on longer, hinting that he was invincible and urging me to get out and about. It was my release and his wish. That day was similar to previous days and Ubac had survived them; I let myself be persuaded by all these reasons that weren't really reasons and decided to go, sure that I'd see him again. And I could believe this, I'd sworn to him that he'd die with his head in my lap, with his pulse gradually dropping away from mine.

I'd put him in the shade in the garden because he could no longer move; I'd told my parents how the sun would shift round from east to west, and explained exactly where they needed to move him to as the hours went by. I'd already told them this a good twenty times, as I had all the other details that they were good enough not to say they already knew. I'd cleaned his tummy and his back end which stank of pee and poo. I'd killed ten flies.

I'd kissed Mathilde who was also heading out and we'd hugged to give each other some courage, each convinced the other had more than ourselves. I'd fiddled about making pointless preparations and didn't say goodbye to my dog properly. Just caught sight of him as I left, no more than that; after a conjoined life, this was the last time, and he knew. I didn't measure up to that moment. This failing still haunts me, it stabs me in the gut, and it's in an attempt to excise it that every evening since then, wherever I am and however obstructive the clouds or the season, I look up to the sky and acknowledge Alnitak, Mintaka and Alnilam, the most 'us' of all the stars.

A few days earlier, Ubac didn't seem to be doing any worse. Death is a downward staircase with half-landings that let you think everything's fine. I could have been worried: Dédé at the Bar d'Arêches once told me that before dying, you rally a bit, sometimes a lot, like a last hurrah. A person is like a rain shower with splashy final droplets reminding the world of their presence and hey presto, perfect stillness.

We spent every day together, so the decline went unnoticed. Yes, there was his hoarse, muted, sepulchral barking; there were minutes on end when he panted loudly as if to the last chaotic beats of a heart; and there were his eyes, so unlike him, impenetrable and icy. He seemed to be capitulating and far from the state of calm people describe. Mathilde and I looked at each other, a good way to avoid his appeals to end it all, and then, because no life – even the most tenuous – is consistent, his would pick up again, perhaps it was coming back. The fierce tension drained away, his breathing eased, he looked rather than stared, he ate a snick of cheese, lapped a few palmfuls of water and seemed very happy for Cordée and Frison to come and cheer up his one square metre of ground. His tail seemed to want to wag again. It perked us up. We humans are so changeable; when life's fading, we can spot its subtlest signs, but if it's there in abundance we ignore it. So, heartened by these small godsends, we delayed the only acceptable decision. We congratulated him for hanging on, the common mistake made by those who'll be left behind when the subject themselves only wants encouragement to let go.

We spent a lot of time cleaning him, tending to him and his suppurating pressure sores. His eyes seemed to say he hated himself for burdening us, and we reassured him that nothing was more important than loving him and being with him. We lived down on the ground, at his level, our heads close together, and we cosseted him without forgetting the other two whom Mathilde or I would take out for a blast of fresh air, an explosion of living creatures running, jumping and racing ahead. We used these opportunities to scream in the woods. They were intense days, they brought us close – not that we needed their help to achieve that.

In the evenings a loving protocol was established: Ubac was clean, had had a bit to eat and had been given a tramadol; Cordée and Frison lay down next to him and so did we; calm descended. We were all doing the same thing at the same time, a now rare trinket of pleasure. The three dogs touched one another with the end of a paw, as if recharging him. There was all the contentment of evening, even though dusk is said to be a time of anxiety. No obvious suffering. Then we got up without a sound, went to the mezzanine and from there we watched them peacefully group themselves together and go to sleep. I think that in our dreams we both hoped it would end like this, in the fading warmth of the household and only four out of five waking. But the very purpose of our dreams is to be courageous in them.

At the beginning of that week, even though we hate diarising, we discussed how it would work. I had to go to Chamonix on the Thursday then write for the next few days, staying at home and devoting myself to it, which was good timing. I insisted Mathilde got away, went to see the sea, ran over the sands of Rivedoux and intoxicated herself on the wind; I wanted her to recharge her batteries with vitality for both of us; together we were getting mired all the deeper. After

hours of negotiations, discussions about the definition of selfishness, considering this life that mustn't
end and the pointlessness of staying put, we agreed
that Thursday was the best day. 'Shh . . .' Mathilde said,
worried Ubac would hear and set his agenda. There was
nothing he couldn't understand. We'd taken to talking
quietly – it was ridiculous.

A few weeks earlier, we'd already been talking about the
end, fears of his death had been lurking.

I wondered whether Ubac was aware of his finite-
ness and how close it was. I think he was – don't animals
in Africa take themselves off to their graveyards? We
knew the summer would be devoted to him, that no
one else could care for him and we'd be permanently
by his side. It went without saying. Summer's a terrible
season for dogs, people abandon them to go and live
their own lives to the full – rescue centres and holes
in the ground fill up. We kept telling him we couldn't
care less about climbing, the warm evenings, or nights
spent outside, he wasn't to sacrifice himself for trifles
like that. We knew it would be a difficult summer, too
bad about trips to Entrèves or Vallouise, there would
be tragedy to face and, from morning till night, the
oppressive feeling that life's tripping by happily everywhere else.

He wasn't a pretty sight; this magnificent dog,
this powerful creature who'd done the rounds of

mountaintops was now just a worn old man who slept all day, his velvety skin reduced to straw-dry parchment; stretches of grey and horrible pasty notches had overrun the pretty pink of his jowls which were now as withered as a forgotten apple; and our reflections dribbled in his drooping eyes. There was nothing I could do for him. Did he know this, or did he think I wasn't using my power to help him?

At the sight of him, I sometimes took refuge in my study to cry copiously. When my eyes were dry again, I'd go over to him with a big smile and he'd look at me as if to say he knew; in the language of the heart, there's no camouflaging anything, just thinking of it is shameful. When our mournful anger at seeing him so incapacitated escalated, we were careful not to direct it at him, and when it erupted from our every pore, we diverted it towards the fucking farmer down the road, a tax demand or, if nothing else came to hand, the limewashed walls where the skin of my fingers spelled out this impotence in bright red initials. Cordée and Frison loved him with all their hearts, they licked him and snuggled up to him. Animals tend to one another in their own way: if a grebe had passed by, it would have draped his tummy in its protective feathers.

We'd hastily built him a sort of bed out of a pallet with a plastic tray to collect his urine without distressing him – he loathed fouling the place. As for poos, there were hardly any now, all solids had disappeared.

We steeped his kibble in water to make a vile broth, but it was the only thing he deigned to eat. Every meal was celebrated as a triumph. Sometimes we carried him outside to give him some fresh air. There were times when we transported him in the van and set him down somewhere else with different views and the two girls bounced around him at a lake or mountain pass or the fringes of a wood that he'd thoroughly explored in the past . . . before my father died, he'd really wanted to see the sea one last time. Right up to the end we were thinking for him. I unleashed my loathing to the first sceptical walker we came across, although I'd promised myself that never in my life would I succumb to that emotion.

We cut ourselves off from the world even more, increasingly unable to cope with the pitying looks of the few people who came to the chalet and seemed to be saying – not that they dared to voice it – that this devastating scene wasn't a life. We couldn't cope with this because it was the truth. The whole place stank of death, and we refused to be brave. We'd always said we would be, that we'd spare him unnecessary overtime, that we'd never let the wrong kind of love make the decisions, and that having dogs offers us the extraordinary luxury, unlike with other people, of protecting them from indignity. In the comfort of his absence, the answer to this question was clear, but when he was there in our faces, all that clarity became hazy.

Ubac and I may have talked about everything, but he'd never mentioned his last wishes.

'We'll take him,' we'd sometimes agreed in the past. 'We owe him that at least, giving him an honourable end, to match the rest of his life.' Neither of us dared to say *put down*, even less *euthanasia* – the words are too cold, metallic. And we said *take him*, which was less of an abandonment. Neither of us dared suggest it to the other now, too worried that, for the rest of our lives, he or she would have prompted Ubac's demise. What a failure. A dog, just by coming into our lives, makes something bigger of them and one gesture would be enough, not to thank him but to raise ourselves to his level. Two syringes, one of nerve and one of dignity, but we were incapable of it, playing on the dubious notion that the injection would be theft. The reality is it would be a leg-up.

And the rhythms of this wretched life helped us to be weak. Ubac regularly became more alert. He had flashes of exuberance and started wanting to catch balls with his mouth, which was soon the only survivor of his paralysis. We saw this as a revival when it might have been just like a senile old man reverting to child-hood games. He barked vigorously in modulations that sounded like happiness and the whole house reso-nated with his return to duty. At the time, the slightest improvement was a victory. Then he would calmly rest his head on my legs, I'd put my hand into his fur which still smelled the same, and our heart rates would slow; the gentleness of it felt good.

I kept thinking of resurrections; surely someone up there would see this rare life force and, by some precise trial by ordeal, they would do their work – there was no harm in hoping. We all felt better when we saw him come alive and could forget, even for a moment, that we weren't up to our task. I'm still wrangling with this cowardice today and I'm afraid of it; we'd both signed a lease that lasted indefinitely.

And what did he think, my beloved Ubac? Was he flattered by our obstinate love? Was he staggered by our selfishness? We ourselves will die without knowing. With Frison and then Cordée we would do things differently: we would do something. Life had taught us to be loyal. Does doing the right thing make you a better person, as is often claimed? I doubt it; it's just a case of switching from being jailor to executioner, and – as far as I know – death doesn't have an agenda for us to live better. We may flail around but in the moment of death we're left with just misplaced anger about all these convictions, however unfaltering they may have been.

A few months earlier, we weren't talking about *deterioration* but *ageing*, it's more palatable. One has a note of darkness, the other of tenderness.

Ubac didn't go so far, so fast, for so long, so often, but that was all. Nevertheless, we avoided some regular activities, some constants, ones whose gradual disintegration would spell out his decline all too clearly. Everything happened slowly, particularly consenting to the idea that he was on a downward spiral. At Lake Saint-Guérin, Cordée and Frison plotted a route all the way round; Ubac turned back at the bridge, pottered from one small achievement to another, and we were all cheerfully united in the end. Mathilde and I, both familiar with different levels of ability in educational settings, laughed about this streaming system and tended to forget that ageing is another thing that happens more quickly in dogs.

The vitality of the other two dogs highlighted Ubac's creakiness but having these distinct generations and energies coexisting made us feel like a clan governed by a wise tribal chief. Sometimes Cordée and Frison would head up the trio, relieving the elder of his surveillance duties, watching over him without usurping his role. Having raised a sort of child and lived alongside a peer, we were now looking after a grandparent. Between meeting and parting there's just a breath and it's important to grab hold of it.

There was no room left for the booster stickers in Ubac's vaccination record and Docteur Fourget proudly started a new one called *Ubac Old*, using the English word which, he claimed, had more oomph to it. He'd been telling us for three years that there hadn't been legions of Bernese Mountain Dogs to hit double figures in his career; I must have signed some sort of pact back in Madame Château's kitchen. Docteur Sanson laughed and told us that when Ubac hit twenty, he'd publish a scientific paper and make a fortune. His smile also told us we shouldn't put too much faith in this eternity.

Ubac couldn't get into the van – his van – by himself any more. And we broke our backs getting him back out. I asked him how he managed to survive with this retired couple – jokes are just one defence against inexorable fate. Then it became normal for us to hold up his hindquarters while he still handled the mobility of his front feet. The briefest walk was now a physical exploit for him and required back supports and ingenuity from us. Everything became noticeably more difficult: the fake marble in Doune's building turned into a real ice rink where he collapsed, his eyes full of apologies; powder snow which had once thrilled him now clogged him like cement. We had to support his rear end for him to relieve himself. Anyone who laughed at this questionable performance – other people's distress is the cheapest source of amusement – would have felt the full force of my contained fury. There was now a disabled member in our microsociety. One of his last vet's appointments took place in the van, in the car park of the Albertville clinic, to spare him a painful move inside and the pathetic spectacle of our questionable love. Fourget's eyes had changed; there was no more laughter, there was no more Mathilde or Cédric.

'You must prepare yourselves, Monsieur and Madame Sapin-Defour.'

From the first day when I grafted this sadness into my life, I'd been doing just that. The thing that was slowly immobilising him couldn't be explained with an -*oma* or an -*itis* against which we could rail. It was just the scars of time, which is a balm or a poison depending on what you want from life.

But there was still an overall contentment. Ubac was there among us.

I occasionally envy older people sitting by the fireside, looking out of the window, reading and going about everything slowly. It strikes me they've been relieved of the tyranny of *doing*, they take time over everything and with gentle conviction they transform their decline into something almost to be savoured. Ubac often gave that impression: he was not so much weary as serenely restful. He could no longer go jumping over rivers and perhaps it was just as well, it made way for the joys of doing nothing or only very slowly. There was no furtive fear of dying. But of no longer living . . .

Ubac was sitting on the ground and, as usual, had his whole weight against my legs, our pulses pressed together and beating faster and faster until the ground reverberated to them. Had our exteriors become more permeable or had our hearts grown larger from so much beating? We didn't ponder that one. There's nothing that the combined effects of hope and wilful blindness can't silence.

Mathilde and I were sure we had a powerful enough love for Ubac to spare him the higher reaches of suffering and disability. We would do what we had to. On the other hand and with equal conviction, we felt that animals knew how to die and, as with so many things, they didn't need our help with it. But for now, on balance, it seemed fine to keep going together. We often played the Pogues' *Pogue Mahone* full blast. Thirteen hymns to a relaunched life encouraging us to keep the dance going and not get wound up about memories. With all this excitement, Ubac would bark and pant all the louder.

One evening there was a faded purple balloon on the breakfast bar in the kitchen – it had the word 'Fiesta' written on it. I don't know what it was doing there but it was just right. I picked it up, put it in front of his mouth and captured his breath; the balloon misted inside, smoothed out its wrinkles and filled slightly. I knotted the end, capturing this parcel of life, and prayed it would be as long as possible before I had to undo it.

A few years earlier, there had been a triumphal carefreeness about Ubac, and a never-ending life had seemed a realistic possibility. Who cared about the future. Like in that poem by Prévert, he was made of 'iron, fire, steel and blood'. Nothing seemed to get the better of him. Ubac was dense, solid, a defensive wall for our little community. When vets shaved some part of him for whatever reason, his fur grew back with lightning speed. We all lived voraciously in the present. The only division of time I was aware of was that there had been before Ubac and now there was Ubac; love cuts life in two.

When we went for walks and he headed up his troop with his proudly barrel chest, some people saw his blazing energy and couldn't help uttering this waste of breath: 'Shame it won't live to an old age.' I told them *it* was called Ubac and their pronouncement was spot on because we saw him staying young for ever. And if these nobodies blundered on with their dark foreboding, we would reply smoothly that this was precisely why we'd got a dog: to be happy for a shorter time.

And we continued on our way.

That was centuries before he died.

How sad and beautiful life would be if we could rewind it like that.

## 21

# The last time

Of course you were dead, the air had changed.

My wretched phone started working again. I called Mathilde and my parents endlessly. It rang in a bottomless void and the next minute I was sent straight to voicemail, to their messages recorded in sunnier times – even minor stories have their golden age. They were right not to pick up, what could they have added, your death notice was clear. But on the way from Chamonix back to Beaufort, from Plan Dernier to the Pacots stream, places where we'd seen so much of life, part of me clung to believing in it and refusing to accept that such a masterwork would end like this.

I reach the chalet and park haphazardly. The front door opens a dog's width, Cordée and Frison race outside and throw themselves at me, fussing, jumping up, scratching and knocking me. Their welcome, which usually draws me inside, acts as a barrier today. Don't go in, he's gone. Their pain may not look like ours, but I mustn't forget it.

Mathilde comes out in tears, with the swollen red face of someone who's spent hours crying. She crosses her hands over each other horizontally several times, the way you indicate giving up in sport – physical gestures are the only means of communicating what's happened. I dreaded this moment thousands of times and now here it is. I wondered what form it would take, would we be alone, would the wind be blowing, would you not make it through a day or a night, what sound would death make, would it fell me on the spot or gradually pull me apart. I pictured where it might happen, but always decided these places were for other things. Except in hopeless situations, no one knows where death lies waiting for them. So it's here that I receive the news, beside a priceless old wooden door with the sun heading westward, surrounded by fussing animals and mute humans. Cars go past on the road as if nothing's happened. Our neighbour Armand waves to me – his day is just a day. What I'd like, I think, is to be struck down on the spot, but that would take more guts than I have.

You're in the middle of the large living room, on the grey bed mat, the most worn one, looking peaceful with your head turned towards the door, lying on your right side, but without the soldier's two red holes in Arthur Rimbaud's tender poem. You didn't die here, that would be impossible, they moved you because of the bastard flies. I'm pleased some of the flies have ended up stuck to the joist tape; the losses on both sides balance out. You could be asleep, there's little to distinguish sleep from death except any hope of waking. But the truth is they're nothing alike. Mathilde and I hug each other tightly, our arms dejected, telling each other, *it's over*, almost *at last*. We soak each other's necks with tears. In the brief moments when we manage to speak, I ask her whether she knows how it happened, what position you were in, what time it was, precisely. Why, when faced with this monumental truth, do we need these tiny details?

I touch you, hug you, ruffle your fur, you're still here. I stroke you all over, brushing the fur the wrong way to make sparks. You feel like you. I'd recognise your smell in the whole of Noah's Ark. How many hours is it before death starts to stink, wiping away the old smells with no warning? If I lie on the floor and line myself up with your face, you look at me, we look at each other, and I'll blink first. Your eyes are wide open. In my memories of westerns, only valiant cowboys died with their eyes open, the baddies' souls couldn't face the world. I hug you close, skin to skin, I smooth out your knotted fur, massage you a bit, hearts have been known to start again. I dream of the land of Thanatos where they simulate death to live in peace.

I go to find my parents, they did their best, and more. We say affectionate things to each other, something we're usually so bad at; one day we won't need grief to have this courage. We cry. With abandon, one after the other – a courtesy, almost a system, which ensures we don't interrupt our loved ones' sobs. In our culture you have to cry, you know, all honourable grieving begins with tears. In church, those who weep for the dead are consoled, regardless of whether they ever wept for them in their lifetime. The dry-eyed are suspect, we see only what's visible. But in this instance, believe me, the tears come from our depths, they were waiting, in waves. We don't resist the urge to cry because within these four walls a dog's death is a tragedy.

Soon we'll be in the outside world with its licences for sadness. In its classification of legitimate pain, losing a dog doesn't rank very high, a long way, a very long way below a child, someone who's lived to a hundred, the unknown soldier, the European turtle dove. Soon there'll be the violent aching void between one side where pain coats everything like lava and the other where the vast majority couldn't care less, don't understand and jeer privately – crying over some animal, how soppy. This gulf obstructs the grieving process by depriving it of its collective rituals; but at the same time, it will help us by bringing us closer, now sure we were right not to trust other people.

Mathilde and I tidy you up, make you presentable. Then we carry you. As we go through the doorway, a splinter of wood snags a few of your hairs, it's the last time you'll be in this place, your home. We lay you down in the car. We take infinite precautions not to hurt you. How many times since I've had to lift you into the car have I complained that you were a dead weight? We've already called Docteur Fourget, he said he was very sorry, and I believe he was. He's expecting you in Ugine. When we have the choice, we avoid this satellite clinic, thinking it grim with its end-of-days paint colour; I think we knew that the conclusion would play out here at some point. Like the pack animals that they are, the other two dogs want to jump in the car. Is it inhumane to leave them here? Is it inhumane to take them with us? My parents rally themselves and pretend to be happy; Cordée and Frison believe them and stay where there's life.

We've positioned you how you like to be in the car, with your head between the front seats. It smells of you. You're here. We turn round several times to see how the journey is for you; the bends at Venthon usually make you sit up, you don't like them, they're too twisty, it's not that you're carsick but you pant, wanting it to be over, getting restless and waiting for the last roundabout at Val des Roses and the straight roads ahead where you lie back down. But today, it's fine, you've accepted them. When Mathilde and I turn round at the same time, we meet each other's eye, and both feel sad for the other's pain. We could drive like this for hours, the three of us, delaying the separation. To think I used to vandalise taxidermists' shop windows and now I'm thinking, stiff or not, at least you'd be there. Is it the meat or the soul that makes the living being? Compared to the rest, to the vastness, the body's not much really, but there would be no movement and without that, nothing looks lifelike.

It's late when we reach the clinic; all the clients have left and that's just as well, we're sparing them their future fears and ourselves their compassionate looks. Fourget is already here. How does he do this work? I don't want him to help us carry you and he knows. He's played this scene hundreds of times, but our experience isn't the umpteenth of anything. I lie you down on the exam-ination table, making a loud thud, two blocks of wood knocking together. I stand by your head as usual, where I can whisper, tell you it's nearly over and you're a good dog. It won't hurt – my usual promise, which will be kept on this occasion.

The vet talks softly as if he's in church. It doesn't suit him, and it doesn't suit you; then the volume increases and it's better. We try to avoid trite phrases, but con-ventions are deeply entrenched. It's for the best, he tells us, and we know, we know there'll never be anything better. I sign a document, perhaps it's been ready for months, like Simone Veil's obituary at *Le Monde*. At the end of the day, I've signed only two documents for you: one in Madame Château's kitchen and one here – dogs are more economical on signatures than children. I point this out to the vet who nods. I almost said, at the end of the dog days – that often happens in all the tumult of sadness, some part of you protects you, could laugh at a feeble pun and never stop. I often get this at funerals, I snort with laughter amongst the tears; I wonder if they incense the dead with laughing gas. And I know that if I ended up laughing out loud here, your brand-new ghost wouldn't be offended, but would see it as a tribute.

Fourget explains what will happen next and it feels better talking logistics. Someone will come to collect you on Thursday, someone anonymous who'll be delivering TVs instead in two months' time. What will you do until then, who'll take care of you? We could have buried you in the garden, under the lupins in Miage, but that would have tied us indefinitely to the house – and it doesn't make any sense for you to prescribe inertia. You'll be cremated. Fourget tells us there are individual cremations and collective ones, and we can choose between a white or a pink bag for you to be put into beforehand. The idea of mingling would suit you – you worked so hard to hybridise other living things – but we opt for you to burn alone, a ridiculous notion of exclusivity, of frightening purity, and also so as not to lose you more fully. I hope the man on Thursday will put your bag into his truck gently; will he have any idea of everything that's inside it?

In a few days we can come and collect a black and gold urn, a cenotaph . . . where will *you* be? It will have some mawkish aphorism about eternity inscribed on it, a cute image, and there'll be a seed to sow, which will grow into a soft pink flower. We won't let you stay in there long, we'll get it done swiftly as Mathilde and I promised each other we would. We'll go up the Aiguille de la Persévérance by the standard route because those are two words – perseverance and standard – were invented for you thanks to your own perseverance and your gift for making anything standard dazzling. We'll open the urn and, buffeted by the North Wind – after all, your name is Ubac – your ashes will be blown to the Aosta valley and beyond, towards the Piedmont mountains. From one horizon to another, wind and pollen fertilizing the world. Some of your dust will fall on the round tables at Relais des Anges where we used to drink Treviso under full moons with your steady presence at our feet. We emerged merry and loose-limbed, our hearts both heavy and light from too much drinking, and you got us back safely.

To sum up, a life is a Tamil *kolam*: we put all our efforts into setting it out in a harmonious geometry, then one day, just after dawn, the wind and the ants disperse its powders, making its transience its most striking beauty. All this is better than rotting under the earth and its frosts.

We keep your collar, your vaccination record and a

tuft of your hair. Later there will be memories but at the moment we need these tools, unguents and instruments of torture. Fourget doesn't make us pay anything, except for the share not intended for him. It's gracious of him – death costs enough as it is, but we wouldn't give a damn if we had to pay a fortune. Equally tactfully, he pretends to go and get something from the next room, leaving us alone. This is the last minute I'll have with you. Or was that this morning? Or was it the last time I saw you run? I think I'd like to die of sadness right here, but to achieve that I'd need a heart as expansive as yours. I look at you ten times to try never to see you like this again; at the risk of losing more than intended, I want to keep only what I've decided to remember. And even though I know we can't dictate how our memory works, I'm stubbornly nudging mine in the right direction. We take great lungfuls of you, I want your smell to be with me for ever. Smell is such an intimate link, not available to others. We leave with a goodbye to Fourget. So that's how these stories end, through a door with a bell on it and with an automatic social nicety. Outside, the world is still obstinately revolving, and I can't get my head around that.

Mathilde and I are tempted to go and get drunk till we lose touch with reality. It would be weak and vital. But we drive back up to the house. We need dogs.

# 22

# Grieving

So what next, my Ubac? I have no idea but I think it'll be tough, extreme, why would our grief be different to any other?

There will be loss. A fierce, organic feeling like a stab in the guts. And that starts this evening in this house which is too big and its ceilings too high, a house we've drained of sap and that echoes emptily. I thought it would be brutal; it'll be worse still. We'll have to weather it; we're assailed by sharp spikes, poking us relentlessly, then they appear to withdraw but they're just lying low, ready to re-emerge, arrogant and pig-headed, as if making us pay for too much happiness. I'll be entitled to writhe and run my tears dry; we have to let our bodies scream their pain because resisting comes at a cost. Not take the pills, not cheat, there's no medicine for this suffering, there shouldn't be any, it's up to the individual to heal.

And starting today, we'll fall asleep at night from too much crying only to wake and for three blissful seconds, at best, we'll have forgotten, our bodies will be at peace. Then thrown back into the fray. I anticipate these wounds, waiting for them, bracing myself, let the fiends take everything I've got, suck out my veins, I won't dodge them, love is an idea that's worth experiencing. And if someone somewhere stops their navel-gazing long enough to suggest – even entertain the thought – that I'm making too much of a fuss and I should see what people are going through in Bangladesh, I'll smash their head in. This won't solve anything except that, by transforming it into pure rage, I will briefly have excised the pain.

There will be the summer and I'll be like the pet who gets left behind.

I'll count the days, I'll think, already! I'll think, is that all? I'll have eyes only for the ugly and the difficult. The adversity everywhere, happier than mine. And the insurmountable shame of having not measured up.

There will be the lost rituals that added up to what our life was: you finishing pots of yoghurt; the *grissini* that had to be snapped into three; you greeting the postwoman; your nose, my elbow, the spilled cup of coffee and the change of clothes; letting you put your front paws on my shoulders and asking you what was the point of standing up like us; filling your barrel of kibble and emptying it one bowlful at a time; our secret promises at bedtime, sleeping near you by the fire and the open shutters, watching you dream of great exploits and battles; the eager mornings; drying you after the rain, your head wreathed in a towel, my trousers streaming; you standing to attention at the sound of a key or your Biscrok gravy bones; you and I both slumped in the van, equally peaceful, watching the busy world go by; idling with our heads in the shade, our bodies in the sun and our backs resting against a wall, massaged by the spirits of the craftsman who laid each stone; me crouching on the ground for you to run at me and bowl me over; lying down in the mountain pastures for a supposedly five-minute siesta that ends up longer, waking with your breath on my face.

No more living on the ground now, back to human level – so that's what the endless tomorrows are offering me. Our days together were no more than this: a heartening protocol peppered with unexpected incidents. How do people fill these minutes with new material? This is how absence goes about its abrasive work: it's a far cry from lyrical illusions about love and death. No, it all boils down to me with a gnarl of Gruyère rind in my hand, devastated that I don't know what to do with it. Do you know the role you played in every waking moment of my days? Being happy together took up all my time – what am I going to do with the sheer bulk of what's been confiscated? We knew in advance, it was foretold, endlessly contaminating our lives: the abyss would be bottomless . . . but what were we supposed to do, hold back? We were stitching our lives together. Remember that Mathilde's grandfather Jean, a weaver with a mischievous twinkle in his eyes, said that you were the weft and I was the warp, and together we made the most tightly woven fabric. A taffeta! That's what he said. The threads bound firmly like armour, but it's all tattered now.

When I had a quick drink on a café terrace and went inside to pay, I used to watch you when you couldn't see me. You were on the lookout, pinning your eyes on the last corner of wall where I'd disappeared and waiting for me to reappear, anxious and trusting. I didn't milk it too much, but that scene filled me with strength. That's all I'll be doing from now on, looking everywhere for those eyes looking everywhere for me.

There'll be coping with seeing you constantly, emerging from every room, from every doorway and after every night, hearing you in every rustle to the point of hallucination. There'll be seeing Mathilde hunched with pain and who, despite the balance we achieved, always thought of herself as second in line for anything to do with you, right down to the rankings of grief. Remind me to tell her every evening that her pain is equal to mine.

There'll be looking in the corners of the house for hairs you shed and breathing the smell of your bedding, drawing on the pain at its source and fighting it hand to hand.

There'll be resenting every dog that's still alive, right down to those – Cordée and Frison – whose lives sustain mine in the toughest times.

There'll be knowing I'm the only male in the pack now but with no illusions of power.

There'll be new places and new people and I'll always wonder what you would have made of them.

There'll be returning to an arid world in which sentimentality's forbidden and there'll be coping with or battling against this world where people shy away from physical contact.

There'll be seeing only an approximation of love, everywhere.

There'll be the universe deprived of your brilliance, and worrying: who's going to recalibrate the world now?

There'll be the piercing conviction that our relationship can't be dissolved or substituted by time.

There'll be waiting to live again, without much faith it'll happen.

There'll be sitting on the ground alone, waiting for Cordée to drink.

And prowling around me will be the deliberate oversights and the temptation not to do everything possible to live. After all, if I don't live so long, we will have spent relatively more days together. I might forget to rope myself at the top of the Aiguille du Peigne; I might cut across drifted snow threatening to avalanche or not make a thing about carcinomas, not so much to tempt fate but to let it choose and see what it has to say about my pathetic lack of nerve to do it myself. There'll be the absence of fear, but not in a boastful way, no fear of the drop below me, of excesses or possibilities; acceptance that it might end. I won't be afraid of anything, not of enthusiasm or boredom. Either I'll burn through life not giving a damn about how it unfolds, or I'll wait and say nothing about how slow it is. In either case, it will be an insult. How will I manage to die if you're not here? But however much I resist it, I will live, new memories will be grafted on, and you won't be in them. I already knew that today and tomorrow won't have any new part of you, but I now realise yesterday won't either.

There'll be the places I can't go to. If I have to, I'll always make a detour via the next path, the next valley or the next planet, but how do you expect me to return to Les Champs and count the nine summer snowfields, or to André's mountain and clear the fallen twigs and leaves from the wash house, or to the Paradis des Praz to dip my feet in icy water? Those wonderful moments of compatibility, those routes we trod together, places permanently marked by your having been there ... they would be hellish – the unliveable part is living again. So I need a change of geography, to leave and never look back or pray that these places vanish in a world turned upside down. In places you never went to, it'll be like the times when I looked forward to coming home to see you and tell you all about it. But you'll be equally absent everywhere, in places loaded with memory just as much as the unfamiliar. Your leaving condemns me to running away with my eyes closed, and you'll play no part in it.

Then, bam, there'll suddenly be no memory of the obligations, the hard work, the shifts keeping watch, the pressure sores to dress, the floor fouled by your old age, the tough times, and your immobility which ensured ours for months. None of that now happened. Your final offering is this reclaimed time and ability to move; well, I don't want it. I won't to do anything with it except feel sickened by the excessive freedom. Anyone want some? I once treasured it, now I'm selling it off cheap. And what about the Crédit Mutuel bank, will it even survive the summer? To think we filled its coffers – with a lot of help from the interest rate – to pay for your treatments. My pointless rage would like to see it, too, collapse.

I'm telling you all this cautiously, my dog. Don't go thinking you're a burden on my life; you unballasted it in so many ways, the balance is eternally in your favour. But it would be wrong to lie to you. I have no clarification about death, that's how befuddling it is, I can't find the right words, are there even any? How to get this across to you . . . Even though I couldn't have loved you any better, I hadn't quite finished loving you.

## 23

# Life goes on

Then one day, with no warning, brighter spells will come along. In the spring most likely.

Before then would be unthinkable. Because there's winter, those short dismal days we struggle to get through. Because no one can make cutbacks in how long it takes for the lighter mornings to return. But one mild day in May, on the south-facing slopes with all their abundance, by who knows what manoeuvre (it certainly won't be intentional), I'll manage to think of you with something like contentment. Probably thanks to the profusion of life before me, the rising breezes, the flowering flowers, the bees reclaiming their land, my warmed body, these communities full of life. For the period of a variation, your absence will have transformed into a sort of melancholy yet consoling substance around me, a cotton-wool shell that envelops, accompanies and protects me.

'You will no longer be where you were but everywhere that I am,' wrote Victor Hugo. Poor man, his invaluable words have been kidnapped by truckloads of death announcements but the idea's right: there's the illusion, which is so powerful it feels real, that I'm not separated from you. Yes, you'll be all around us, wrapped around our days; it wouldn't take much to touch you. It will now be possible to talk to you without wailing, I'll go back to believing how support-ive ghosts can be and, even though you never did it in your lifetime, you'll answer when I speak to you – you'll be the most alive of all absentees.

I thought I was destined to sadness for ever and will emerge from it haphazardly, stunned to be breath-ing again and to discover that everything is tempor-ary, even torpor. On intrepid days I'll be able to look at photos of you beside the little stone outbuilding at Le Châtelet, one in which you adopted a powerful pose with your face in the sun, the only picture I know that so strikingly and lastingly shows your combination of calm and alertness. I'll be able to watch the thirty-seven-second film of you bounding through the snow one December, destined for a great future. I'll manage to look the past in the face, to accept everything it serves up unfiltered, and to love it as it deserves to be loved, because it's what's left in the present and so it deserves a lot. I'll feel as if I've always known you. The hardest thing will be recordings of your voice when you growled to make yourself sound fierce and when you howled with excitement. I still won't cope with them because sound revives the illusion of a presence more powerfully than images.

In this place where we live surrounded by nature, I'll find you in another dog's features, in the bark of a puppy born around mid-July, in the soaring flight of an eagle or the creak of a larch. Your spirit will be there, and your strength. Not every time because, like anything forced, it wouldn't ring true; and never by chance but it will be sufficiently rare to have meaning. Then the others in my rope team will catch me whispering to the cirrhus clouds and teetering cairns, but they won't worry about it because they've been there a long time and individuals along the same length of rope would never twist it with any sort of judgement. Quite the opposite, in fact: they'll think that this receptivity to mists and stones announces the chutzpah and progress of the future. The tears that break through will feel gentler on my cheeks, almost warm. Cordée will learn to drink alone.

Inactive until now, consolation will start to get the upper hand over dejection. I'll tell myself to live happily as you always did, not to be what you wouldn't want me to be, stubbornly gloomy since July, not to see your death (because I'll finally be able to call it that) as an end in itself but to view you as such a significant temporary feature that you'll always remain. And these mantras will gradually do their work inside me, changing me for real until they've established a system for feeling better.

On the steep slopes of the Mirantin, with snow up to my knees, I'll remember your energy and I'll emerge at the top by the sunlit peak rather than letting myself be wreathed in shadows. I'll get my breath back. Basically – and it's a dizzying undertaking – I'll try to heave myself up to your level. They say time heals everything, and it's so mindlessly true. The tick and tock of it measure and forge human beings far better than we ever could. At times it will work very well and will be enough to provide happiness; at others, it will be a total failure aggravated by my guilt for having dared to master my sadness.

In the very early days, we'll go about it deliberately, methodically: we'll refuse to lose hope in life, more out of discipline than conviction. That will be a time of unpredictably black or white days, depending on the pendulum swing of our spirits. Then it will start to be second nature, but we'll have to step into this life warily.

On glorious sunny days and surrounded by cheerful people, we'll make pilgrimages to the woods at Le Pellaz to forage for chanterelles or to Félicien to stir up pleasant memories of his coffee for 'four forty'. We'll touch walls that you touched and tread on newly sprung growth on whose ancestors you once lay. We'll chat like old-timers, saying, Do you remember Ubac? And how! Yes, I remember him. I knew that life. You never know, we might laugh about the time you had a stick in your mouth and got stuck trying to pass between two ash trees, or when you went prospecting under the skirts of various ladies, including our neighbour who didn't like it and Jacqueline who didn't say anything. Sometimes, we'll tumble back down and come running home in tears.

On bad nights, I'll picture you as a stray, alone and dirty on the dark roads around Maramurş in Romania, your eyes averted, avoiding uncaring humans. But overall, we'll make progress, good memories will steadily take up residence and we'll be capable of living well. Sometimes I'll dream again; oh, just little dreams, the sort that don't break your heart when you wake. The pain won't have been tamed; we will have come to an understanding, a compromise – it's a start.

We'll prefer spending time with people you loved, but given that you loved everyone, we'll tend towards those who talk about you accurately and who loved you back, particularly Jako. As for the others, if they didn't understand the highs, what hope is there for them to be sensitive about the lows. Their loss.

We'll manage to enjoy ourselves again; to gather fistfuls of arbutus berries on the Aiguilles de Bavella, and with careful finger work pick alexanders in Saint-Clément; to say yes to celebrations; to make our way through the chilly valleys of Planpincieux; to dance on the beach till the fishing boats come home; to bite greedily into Ljubljana's *štruklji*; to spiral through the blue sky's thermals; to climb granite facades again; to raise a glass of Valpolicella in a tight-knit group with Sylvain, Jean-Mi, Soph, Seb and the others; to laugh out loud at one of their blunders; to show due concern for another one's problems; to throw a ball for the insistent Cordée; to chase after the mischievous Frison; to love them for themselves; to grumble cheerfully about the stupidity of people who talk loudly and drive fast; to watch tenderly as our parents grow old; to love letting the wind buffet our hair; to sway to Compay Segundo; to walk in forests; to read Thoreau glorifying creatures that walk in forests; and to laugh hard enough to lose our eyes in creases.

We'll persevere like this until we rediscover how innocence operates, and then we'll be receptive again, infinitely receptive to the world's beauty. We'll grant ourselves sunshine and the silence of horizons; we'll bag anything that shines, we'll even have plans, we'll say yes to life. The story of happiness is impossible to tell, and it may be only a holiday from pain.

From avoiding seeing them, I'll now be able to spot them everywhere: rock coloured and crouching low at an altitude of a thousand metres; on the pavement opposite, parked between happy legs; a head on a balcony; or a wake on the lake. Dogs. We develop a raptor's keen eyesight for the things we love; I'd packed mine away but will start using it again. I'll detect their presence, we'll make eye contact. I'll know when to go ahead and when to postpone, when to talk to them and when not, when to reach out a hand and when to back down. As if reconciled with an extra sense. And when a stranger's dog wants a cuddle, I won't say no – after all, they haven't done anything wrong. When I touch them, I'll be touching two dogs. Perhaps one of them will pass on a message.

There will be minutes when I forget you. No, this won't be the oblivion people talk about, that's not where to draw the strength to carry on, but – tactfully and with no slamming doors – you'll absent yourself from my thoughts. Your first disappearances will be just a few seconds, facilitated by activity, a crowd, clear skies or a waffling conversation. Then hours and nights, even when I'm doing nothing, even in silence. And then you'll gently reintegrate my thoughts, or you'll crash back into them depending on the mood of the day. Basically, we'll be companions again, spending just the right amount of time together, when the feeling takes us, and leaving each other space.

But there will be definite setbacks. At times and in inconvenient places, I'll have 'rivers on my cheeks' as the song by Alain Souchon goes. They'll be great tides as a result of not crying for a week, and they'll feel never-ending, making me think that the sharp, fulsome, vengeful pangs of the early days are back – and why shouldn't they be? I'll accept them willingly – go ahead, flay me again. Take what comes, Grandpa Lulu used to say, life ebbs and flows. It might happen in the middle of the Year 7 dance class set to hideous American music, there's no knowing. It might happen in a place that's so new and so beautiful but so devoid of you, there's no knowing.

Then the tides will calm. And become less frequent. Until I worry that they've gone for good. Who hasn't felt anxiety about an absence becoming absent? Some days, to ward off this fear of forgetting, I'll stir up the embers of my sadness, turning for help to Orion, the six-note riff of Jean-Louis Aubert's 'Alter Ego' or some other tear-duct stimulant. Then I'll think better of this indecent behaviour. People around me will say, Hey, you seem to be doing okay, and I may find myself acknowledging that it's true. This reaching towards brighter days is called grieving by the Church and in medicine; and it can be seen either as a wonderful celebration of life or contemptible selfishness. We have to let it come and do its work, not turn our backs on it; see it as a transition we can't fulfil without a degree of conviction. Without its help, no part of the future is imaginable. A few zealous adherents subscribe to the noble idea of suffering for life, but by its very essence, true suffering doesn't last. It kills, dwindles or changes.

As for you in all this, dear Ubac, in all these qualms

expressed by a man who was raised on procrastina-
tion and is worried about being happy, I hope you just
don't care. Maybe you're already playing with Pirate,
Tchoumi and other mutts, hopping from a tree into a
soul, from one body into another. I don't know what
substance you're made of now – it must be solid and
vaporous – but whatever it is, I know you're watching
over us (and that dopey belief would have infuriated
me before).

Moving from lulls in the storm to brighter spells, the
four of us – Mathilde, Cordée, Frison and I – will have
made our way through a year as singletons. We will
have tackled birthdays of mine in April and Mathilde's in September, the stags roaring, Mathilde's grandmother Simone turning a hundred, first snows, days
like any other but that people make films about, days
when we know exactly who's missing and we start to
dread some dates just as much as we once cherished
them. And those wretched days don't deserve anything,
not dancing or crying or putting fresh flowers on a
grave. They warrant being treated like all the rest. But
however actively we try to neglect them, the tear-off
calendar unfailingly launches its attack. So, when we
come to 13 July for the first time, we'll avoid any artifice,
we'll go up into the mountains where we can howl
without disturbing anyone and we'll cry rivers – the

neighbouring mountaintops will think someone's summited. For future anniversaries, we'll just have to see. Who knows, one of these summers we may spend 13 July without any trouble because, yes, there will also be the comforting, unspeakable hope of not giving a damn.

# 24

# Thanks to you

One clear autumn morning in the middle of all this passing time, I'll walk the Pas d'Outray trail in the mountains.

You loved autumn, I know you did, it was a season that suited you. It's when the weather starts to get colder and you didn't seek out the shade so much, we spent less time in the mountains, returned home earlier, and your rolling around in fallen leaves foreshadowed escapades in the snow. On 4 October we'd buy you a birthday box of junk food which made your breath smell for two full days – we pinched our noses, and you just licked us harder.

You loved Pas d'Outray. On the way there, we passed the Croës Patisserie; we'd double-park and buy Cyril's praline-flavoured *financiers*. At first, we cut them in three, then four, then five, and at that point we bought an extra one. Up at Plan du Mont, there were roe deer skipping and bucking, slightly drunk from eating too many fermented berries. In the dark woods filled with magical sounds, you set off as our pathfinder, saying hello to the ghosts until we reached Hauteluce and were back in daylight. After the marmot-populated scree that damaged your paws, you were back on the short grass of the Pas and you rolled on it like a roly-poly toy, then raced to a pond of cool water. *Saucisson* skins left by hunters eating at Les Trois Moineaux – where everything's cooked but nothing's hot – didn't last long.

On limitless days, we'd keep going on the flat to the Lac Noir where, if confirmation were needed, you demonstrated yet again that you hated being more than knee-deep in water. We sat on the shores, having a break and looking at the view. Moments like that seem so straightforward, almost a gift, but we can't savour them unless every aspect of life is included in them – the truth is they're achieved. Some days we'd get home in darkness, with Mont Blanc glowing pink behind us, happy on tiredness and solitude. It's a beautiful spot up there and it makes you want to return to it from anywhere in the world.

So I'll go up there and make the most of some vital moments alone. The vegetation will be green and red, depending on the leaves and thorns, the sky will be an exuberant blue, and the highest peaks dusted with new white, plotting the onset of winter. The *katabatic* wind will make the woods shivery cold, and further up the inverted weather pattern will see me put away my woolly hat while Beaufort is cloaked in mist. The autumn's great, it's hot but not sweltering and the light's just right. The autumn will always be great but we won't look forward to it together any more. The first chamois that lets me catch a glimpse of it will be very like you, we'll give each other a wave. I'll extend the circular walk to spend longer with the memory of you. I'll go to Les Enclaves and all the way to the shores of the lake, behind the rock shaped like a camel's head. I'll sluice some water over my face, the dark water you used to drink, and I'll see myself reflected in it.

And do you know who I'll see there? A happy man. Conscious of his inheritance and of the spectacular change of direction his life has taken. A happy man who has no problem with being happy.

And that's thanks to you, Ubac, and to the two little things you brought into my life, like presents left casually on the corner of a table, secretly and without any song and dance. A battery and a key. These small objects may not look like much, but they keep me going.

You were born for love, a subtle love that's neither blind nor captive, and you grafted a tiny electric something under my skin that watches over my heart and stimulates it to behave in the same way. I watched you live, and your perception of the world spread to me. You didn't just go hand in hand with this love, it was more than that: you generated it and you equipped me with it – if it weren't for you, it would have passed me by. You showed me that we have to dare to love, always, whether it's ambient love or resplendent love, never prevaricating, never waiting for reciprocation or giving in to the idea that it rewards less than it costs. I adapt this truth to my human life, but I make myself adhere to it every day, not by copying you like some obsessive disciple but in a way of life that, despite the relapses, is becoming second nature.

'What if we taught love?' an art teacher colleague of mine once asked when he was disillusioned by the chilly formality of education. Another colleague said that things like that can't be taught, and I'm now in a position to object and say that they can at least be learned.

The other thing you left me is a small, unpolished, forged key whose blade looks like a reflection of the Tre Cime di Lavaredo, the key to a door that I can open whenever I feel like it, as soon as the human world becomes too much of a scrum. I could be with a rowdy tableful of people, in the razzle-dazzle of cheering, the rumblings of a housing estate or the grey office of some bigwig, the door's always there, open to me and hidden from others. To open it I don't need to inject myself with anything; with training, I need only take a deep breath and blink my eyes. The door leads on to a little side street and a haven formed by fallen trees where I can talk to the clouds, to fox cubs and to invisible creatures. It's a place that's both denser and lighter, a place of wisdom and madness, of resistance and abandon, a fortress with no walls and no morals.

I can go there whenever I need to; I feel good there, instantly, and can celebrate a discreetly impetuous life. When I'm there, I can withdraw from the world for a minute or several days, stripping away everything superfluous, recharging myself so that my pulse rate drops and my soul soars. It's invigorating and very addictive, and no one notices I've gone. There are no humans there but plenty of other living things, and I re-emerge from this back room feeling wonderful, ready to take on the giddying world again, welcoming all that's beautiful and good but also supremely exacting. I see life – which hasn't changed much – as if through clear water; everything is slightly distorted but profoundly limpid, and if some truth bigger than me were ever questioned, I'd know exactly which pebble to reach for.

You taught me these bridges; without you, I would never have gone looking at a day from the other side. And, although I make only modest claims to be a part of this vaster universe, visiting it every now and then infuses everything with lucid and serene beauty. In the official world, the one we're born into, the tangible one with diagrams and deltoid muscles and documentation – and which can be a lovely world – I come across people whose eyes tell me they too know this magic land, on the margins and with no frontier, where the only valid possibility is to listen out for what we're missing, things that don't really exist but in their simple honourable qualities make better individuals of us. These people seem to have found their rightful place; they tread lightly over the ground, and their eyes are those of the well-travelled who may make their getaway at any moment. We smile at each other when we meet, as if saying *alleluia* and *shush*.

The better things are, the more I wonder why humans feel such a need for beeps and whirligigs to augment their reality. The better things are, the more I wonder which of these two worlds is the real one.

So, my dog, equipped with these things – a battery and a key – life can go on, impervious to slumps. You could have screwed it up smaller, but you opened it out wider, and you didn't come into it by chance, there was method and urgency. The dance of who's supporting who is a funny thing: it was you, my four-footed friend, who got me on to my own two feet. For these aptitudes and for other traces of your time here that I'm yet to discover, I say thank you – what other words are there?

Not long ago, in a spent-far-too-long-waiting room, I read a beautiful article about the almost vanished art of illuminating manuscripts. Using less flashy material than gold, that's what you did and still do: you embellished my small existence with elegant touches. Our life together deserves better than finding pretty words for it, but *illuminator* suits you so well.

*

Then I'll go to Pas d'Outray again. The sheep will have come back down the mountain, and I'll be able to drink the water in the stream safely. I'll wait for a southerly wind to surge up the Les Villes slope, I'll let my sail fill and go up to join the buzzards again. Time won't weigh heavily on me, I'll go back home, life will reek of love the way your mouth always reeked on 4 October.

And there at the house, under Lulu's desk, will be the balloon. The one with your air in it. It will look more inflated, not for the first time. This isn't because life around it has depreciated, but because your breath is still obstinately keeping it alive from the inside.

I'll be tempted, as I am every time, to undo the knot, release it, aerate myself with it and breathe you in. But I'll wait a little longer.

So that as much of you as possible keeps going.